Fruit Lovers' Devotions to Go

Nourish Your Body & Sweeten Your Spirit

Beth Bence Reinke

Lisa —
" Sweet " blessings to you !!
Beth Bence Reinke
2013

All Scripture quotations, unless otherwise indicated, are taken from the *Holy Bible, New International* Version, ® NIV. Copyright © 1973, 1978, 1984 by International Bible Society. Used by permission of Zondervan Publishing House. All rights reserved

Published by See Media, Inc.

Carson City, NV

ISBN: 978-1-934626-25-2
Printed in the United States of America

Dedication

With love and appreciation to my heavenly Father.

With eternal thanks to Madge Gulley and Ruth Horner for introducing me to Jesus when I was a little girl.

Fruit Lovers' Devotions to Go

Introduction

Dear Friend,

As a dietitian, I often talk with other women about nutrition and health. Many busy moms express shame about serving convenience foods for supper or hitting the drive thru while shuttling kids to and fro. Instead of fretting over imperfect dinnertime decisions, I recommend a simple change that transforms guilt into joy – just add fruit! It's pretty and colorful and tastes oh-so-sweet.

Adding fruit is an easy, natural way to improve the nutrition of any meal your family eats. There are zillions of ways to do it. Toss berries into a salad or oatmeal. Add dried fruit to cookies or quick breads. Pack fruit into plastic zipper bags to take with you in the car. One of my favorite tricks is to put a serving of fresh fruit at each person's place before breakfast or supper. When it's the first thing they see, kids (and husbands) gobble it up.

The thirty devotions in this book touch on many physical and spiritual aspects of fruit: the health benefits of eating it, fruit-related tales from my life as a mom, ideas for developing fruit of the spirit inside ourselves and encouragement for bearing fruit outside ourselves. Each reading gives you a kitchen-tested fruit recipe to make for your family.

Fruit is mentioned almost two hundred times in the Bible. Words and phrases such as "fruitful," "fruit-bearing" and "fruit of the spirit" are used throughout scripture to describe a fulfilling, abundant life. I hope these devotions give you fresh, fruitful insights and inspire you to become fruit-filled in body and spirit. Remember...just add fruit!

Blessings,
Beth
www.bethbencereinke.com

#1
Party in a Bowl

*Dear friends, I pray that you may enjoy good health and that
all may go well with you*
3 John 2a

Sometimes my fond memories of special occasions include foods, like fruit. Picking cherries with my family. Juicy watermelon wedges at a fourth of July picnic. Hot apple cider after a hayride. Homemade cranberry sauce at Thanksgiving.

One of my favorite fruit-related memories was actually caught on film. When my older son, Ben, was a toddler, he played with a plastic bandage box with a flip-top lid. He loved to put diced apples in the box so he could flip the lid open, eat a bite, then snap it shut. I cored, peeled and cut many apples in those days because Ben took the little box everywhere.

When he was almost two, Ben wouldn't sit still during our family portrait, so we let him hold his apple box. In the photo, you can see the box at the bottom of the picture. Instead of a smile, Ben had a chipmunk cheek because he stuffed it with apple chunks right before the photographer snapped the shot!

I have cut up hundreds and hundreds of apples since then, for Ben's little box and for many bowls of fruit salad served to family and friends. Making fruit salad requires time and effort, but for me it's a labor of love. I love the variety of colors - bright orange cantaloupe, ruby red berries, vivid green kiwis and grapes.

The best part of making fruit salad is when the fruit is cut up and it's time to stir it all together. The spoon dips up and down like a Ferris wheel, blending the fruits into a kaleidoscope of colors and textures. Mmm, can't you just taste it? There's something joyful about fruit salad. It's like a party in a bowl!

God must have had fun creating all the different varieties of fruits that grow on trees, vines and bushes. He packaged fruits in such creative ways. Grapes grow tightly clustered in big bunches. Peaches have soft, fuzzy skin while pineapple skin is rough and scratchy, topped with a stiff green crown. Melons are encircled in a hard, thick rind that makes a "thunk" when you knock on it. No matter what their shapes or sizes, fruits add pizzazz to any meal.

Since the Garden of Eden, people have been sustained by the natural, life-giving nutrients in fruit. Each fruit is a lovingly-prepared health tonic from God - full of essential vitamins and minerals along with a hefty dose of fiber. He even designed it to taste juicy and sweet so even the pickiest of eaters would enjoy it. Can you imagine Adam and Eve tasting each kind of fruit for the first time? What fun that must have been!

Fruit is also bursting with antioxidants, powerful plant compounds that protect health by fighting harmful molecules called free radicals. Scientists continue to study antioxidants to learn more about the special jobs they do inside our bodies. Fruit is truly one of God's best provisions for promoting vibrant health.

Got fruit? If not, stop at the grocery store to stock up. Surprise your family with a sweet, colorful "party in a bowl" with dinner.

Prayer: Thank you, Lord, for your provision of beautiful, sweet fruit. As I begin this journey of putting more fruit on my table, help me to be open to the spiritual aspect of fruit, too. In Jesus' name, Amen.

Honey-Kissed Fruit Salad

Ingredients:

1 cantaloupe, cut into 1-inch cubes
2 pounds strawberries, cut in halves or quarters
1-1/2 pounds green grapes
3 kiwis, peeled and sliced

Dressing:
1/4 cup honey
1/4 cup orange juice
1/4 teaspoon cinnamon

Directions:

Toss cantaloupe, strawberries and grapes in large bowl. Mix dressing ingredients in a liquid measuring cup and stir with fork until blended. Drizzle dressing over fruit and stir well. Arrange kiwi slices on top. Serves 10-12.

This is a great dish for parties, potlucks or family dinners. You can skip the dressing and enjoy the fruit "unadorned" if you prefer.

#2
Fruit of the Spirit

But the fruit of the Spirit is love, joy, peace, patience,
kindness, goodness, faithfulness, gentleness and self-control.
Galatians 5:22-23

Most of us want to have positive personality traits like kindness and patience. The Bible has a name for these good characteristics that are listed in today's verse – the fruit of the spirit.

Wouldn't it be nice to have a tree in the backyard full of these fruits? If you feel stressed, just pick some peace-fruit to have for breakfast. Stash a patience-fruit in your lunch bag to take to the office or grab a self-control-fruit to help you skip dessert. Unfortunately, no such tree exists.

Perhaps studying fruit trees can give us insights about fruit of the spirit though. Fruit doesn't just pop out on a tree instantly. The tree spends a long time getting ready to produce the external fruit. The roots spend months soaking up nutrients from the soil. For weeks the tree drinks rain and absorbs warmth and light from the sun. But even then, fruit still doesn't magically appear. It takes even more time for the nutrients to be drawn up the trunk and through the branches to the leaves. It takes time for blossoms to form and bees to pollinate them. Finally, after months of preparation, the tree is ready to work on growing the external fruit.

You and I are like fruit trees. Just like the tree needs time to absorb water, nutrients and sunlight, we need lots of time to incorporate the "fruit of the spirit" qualities into our personalities. Fruit of the spirit is an internal development. It's about the state of our hearts. When we're making progress by becoming more patient or more kind, we are developing "internal fruit."

So how do we acquire these character traits called fruit of the spirit? I don't know about you, but good characteristics like gentleness, peace and patience don't come naturally to me. I need all the help I can get! Since all good things come from God, asking Him for help is the best place to start.

For me, building fruit of the spirit into my personality requires prayer and practice. First, I ask God to help me cultivate the particular character trait. Second, I practice the trait by trying specific changes. For instance, to practice gentleness, I might try disciplining my kids in a soft voice instead of a drill sergeant imitation. Pretty soon, I speak softly more often than I yell.

In addition to much prayer and much practice, developing the fruit of the spirit takes much time. It's a constant process of learning about each character trait and trying to incorporate it into everyday life. The goal is not perfection, so making mistakes along the way is to be expected.

Developing fruit of the spirit isn't meant to be another self-improvement scheme or one more item for the to-do list. It is a way to nurture your spirit, allowing the positive traits to blossom and grow. Learning new ways of interacting with your family and friends can enhance your relationships and increase your joy. It feels wonderful to know you're cultivating the character traits God intends you to have.

Each of the next nine devotions talks about one of the character qualities called fruit of the spirit. For each one, we can pray for God's guidance, then practice making changes in our behavior. Will you join me in the ongoing pursuit of spiritual fruit?

Prayer: Dear God, please help me to learn about fruit of the spirit. Guide me as I begin to incorporate these qualities into my life. In Jesus' name, Amen.

Fruited Beef Roast

Ingredients:

3-pound chuck roast
2 tablespoons olive oil
2 cups mixed dried fruits, finely chopped
1/2 cup hot water
1 large sweet onion, finely chopped
2 large carrots, finely chopped
1/2 cup red cooking wine
1/2 teaspoon salt
2-4 tablespoons flour
1/4 cup cold water

Directions:

Place dried fruits in bowl and pour hot water over them. Set aside for 30 minutes, stirring occasionally. Heat olive oil in pan over medium heat. Brown roast in oil and place in crock pot. Pour mixed fruits, onion, carrots, garlic and cooking wine over roast. Sprinkle salt over all ingredients. Cook on low for about 6 hours or high for about 4 hours.

Place roast on a serving platter, leaving fruit and juices in crock pot. Add 2-4 tablespoons flour to 1/4 cup cold water and stir with a fork until blended. Pour into crock pot and stir briskly until sauce thickens. Spoon fruit and sauce over beef.

This roast cooks up melt-in-your-mouth tender and flavorful. The thick fruit and veggie sauce is savory sweet and makes a great topping for brown rice.

#3
Love is a Doing Word

Be devoted to one another in brotherly love.
Romans 12:10

Do you remember learning about nouns and verbs in elementary school? I still remember my teacher saying, "A noun is a person, place or thing. A verb is a "doing" word." Grammatically speaking, the word "love" can be either a noun or a verb, depending on the context.

When we talk about the fruit of the spirit though, love is a "doing word." It's something we do. More importantly, love is something we *choose* to do. Loving other people through our words and actions is one of the most important jobs we have in this world.

Jesus knew how to love people. He showed love to others in practical ways like healing with a touch, providing food and calming their fears. He even kneeled on the floor and washed the disciples' feet. Fruit-of-the-spirit love is not a passive affection that waves from a distance and holds up a sign that says "I love you." To love the way Jesus did, we need to be intentional about looking for tangible ways to care for our family, friends and even strangers.

Have you ever felt loved by the way someone treated you? A time when I was given special consideration during an ordinary errand left a lasting impression on me. I stopped by the local public high school to pick up some paperwork. It was my first visit to the building, so I was nervous about following security procedures and finding the proper staff member's office.

In the school's main office, a friend I hadn't seen in months jumped up from her desk and hurried over to hug me. Lori smiled, patiently explained the sign-in process and gave me a visitor sticker. We chatted about our families, then she escorted me through the hallways to the proper office and introduced me to the lady I needed to see. What could have been a nerve-wracking errand turned into a joyful catch-up session. I felt completely cared for as Lori provided friendly guidance in an unfamiliar place.

Even though she probably didn't realize it, Lori modeled the love of Jesus to me that day. I wondered, "Do I take the time to truly focus on others during my busy day like she did?" As women, we have so many people who need us – husbands, kids, parents, friends, coworkers and more. How can we possibly have enough love to go around? If we try to love everyone just in our own strength, we simply can't do it.

The secret is to allow God to love us first, then allow His love to flow through us to others. When we first realize how much God loves us, it's overwhelming. It's a jumble of emotions – amazement, humility and eventually empowerment. We feel so grateful for His love that we want to fully experience it and pass it on to others.

Think about the people in your life. Does a girlfriend or coworker need someone to dote on her a little? Have you spent time cherishing your husband or devoting your full attention to your child? Be intentional. Plan a way to make someone feel loved today.

Prayer: Dear Lord, thank you for loving me. Help me find opportunities to show fruit-of-the-spirit love to others. In Jesus' name, Amen.

Strawberry-Mango Salsa

Ingredients:

1 pound strawberries, diced
1 large, firm mango, diced
1/4 cup thinly sliced green onions
2-3 tablespoons fresh cilantro, chopped
2 teaspoons lime juice
2 tablespoons orange juice
1 teaspoon balsamic vinegar
1/4 teaspoon salt

Directions:

Place fruit, onion and cilantro in medium bowl and stir together. Mix juices, vinegar and salt in liquid measuring cup and blend well. Pour over fruit mixture and stir well to blend. Serve with tortilla or corn chips. Makes 3 cups. Use within 1-2 days.

From kids to grandparents, everyone loves this refreshing salsa. Delicious with chicken or as a salad topper.

#4
Battle of Joy

...for the joy of the Lord is your strength.
Nehemiah 8:10b

Most battles are not joyful, but there is one exception. At our house we do a crazy thing called a "ball battle" which is pure pandemonium. I love to see the joy in my sons' grins as they initiate the chaos.

Ball battles usually begin when my unsuspecting husband is relaxing in the easy chair, his back to the hallway. The boys fetch their stash of ammunition: a tall, plastic bucket filled with foam balls of all shapes and sizes. They sneak down the hall, silently stuffing their t-shirt fronts with balls. On cue, they give a war whoop and simultaneously pummel my husband with the cushy balls. He gathers up strays and hurls them back. Everyone scrambles to grab loose balls and strike back over and over.

Balls fly helter-skelter for ten minutes, coupled with rolling-on-the-floor, gut-busting laughter when players hit their intended targets. It's even more fun when the boys have friends over and they join in the skirmish. After all, how often do kids get to throw things at a grown-up?

It's important to build joy into our lives by doing fun activities with family and friends. Sharing joy enriches our lives and draws us closer to loved ones. But as much as my family enjoys a ball battle, it's only a short-lived high of giggles and belly laughs. When the balls are stowed back in the bucket, the battle is just a happy memory.

Thankfully, there is a special type of joy that never ends. It's called the "joy of the Lord" and comes from having Jesus as your savior. Knowing your sins are forgiven and you'll go to heaven someday brings a deep sense of trust in the Lord's goodness.

The joy of the Lord strengthens us for struggles, burdens or grief that may lie ahead. Even when life gets really, really hard, this kind of joy hangs tough. It nestles deep down in your heart to sustain you during good times and bad.

The apostle Paul had joy even though he spent years as a destitute prisoner. The joy of the Lord gave him the strength to endure being chained to a guard day and night. He kept his heart and mind focused on God, not his circumstances. It brought him joy to share his faith with his guards or anyone else who would listen. Joy in shackles - amazing, isn't it?

The most joyful person I know is my friend, Nelian, who is a missionary in the United States and her native Philippines. She's quick to offer a hug and her smile is radiant. Nelian's love for Jesus bubbles up in her speech as she praises Him for every little good thing in her life. She has joy whether enjoying the comforts of home or ministering in an area without electricity or running water. The joy of the Lord penetrates Nelian's heart and influences her response to every person and situation she encounters.

What kind of joy do you have? Is it the kind that ebbs and flows like ocean waves on the sand - surging forward then draining away? If your joy is based on circumstances around you, it will come and go with the ups and downs of living. But when you look to Jesus as your hope and confidence for the future, real joy settles in to stay.

Prayer: Dear Lord, thank you for making indescribable joy available to me through Jesus. In His name, Amen.

Orange Cream Popsicles

Ingredients:

2 cups cantaloupe, cubed
1 cup orange sherbet
1 (6-ounce) container custard-style vanilla yogurt

Directions:

Place cantaloupe in blender or food processor and blend until purée consistency. Add sherbet and yogurt and blend well. Pour into popsicle molds, insert sticks and freeze. Makes 6-8 popsicles.

These taste a lot like the boxed ones but contain way more nutrients and even a little fiber.

#5
Rules for Peace

*Do not be anxious about anything, but in everything, by
prayer and petition, with thanksgiving, present your requests
to God. And the peace of God, which transcends all
understanding, will guard your hearts and your minds in
Christ Jesus.*
Philippians 4:6-7

One morning I spied a sheet of yellow construction paper
taped to my younger son's bedroom door. In his elementary
printing it said:

Rules are:

One or two toys out at a time.
Don't argue at all.
Don't break toys.
And don't sin or be mean.

Such wise words from a little boy, I thought. Whether the
rules were aimed at his friends or his older brother, Joey
wanted his room to be a place of peace and harmony.

Do you ever wish for peace in your heart and your home?
Working a job, shuttling kids and keeping clothes and toilets
clean in between leads to a frayed feeling, like a rope stretched
taut and unraveling bit by bit. Constant stress and anxiety fuel
only exhaustion and it's hard to have peace when you're
running on empty. I wish filling our hearts and homes with
peace was as easy as pumping gas into our cars.

To help us find more of this intangible fruit of the spirit, the apostle Paul wrote some "rules for peace" that we can apply. Let's break down today's verses, piece by piece, to find his suggestions.

Rule #1: Don't worry. The verse says "Do not be anxious about anything." Oh my, that's a hard one, isn't it? Even though there is much to fear in this world, God doesn't want us to fret. The first step toward peace is relinquishing control - letting go of your will and wishes. Peace comes when we realize that God is in control, not us. He's a big, big God and can handle anything!

Rule #2: Pray. The verse continues: "but in everything, by prayer and petition, with thanksgiving, present your requests to God." He cares about every little detail of your life. When you feel yourself tensing up with worry, take a deep breath and surrender your concern to God. Thank Him for His blessings and tell Him your needs and the needs of others. God is your loving Father who longs to hear your voice.

Rule #3: Rejoice. We're encouraged to pray "with thanksgiving." Being thankful puts the focus on God and the blessings He has given you. Speaking your gratefulness out loud is a wonderful way to help your kids learn to be thankful.

The last part of the verse is the best: "And the peace of God, which transcends all understanding, will guard your hearts and your minds in Christ Jesus." It means that when you believe in Jesus and do those three things, a supernatural peace will come over you. This incredible peace is beyond what our human minds can comprehend. It protects our hearts and minds to keep anxiety from sneaking back in.

Peace becomes contagious when we model it for our families. There is a plaque that reads: "When Mama ain't happy, ain't nobody happy." That's spot on, but the opposite is true, too. When Mama is happy, everybody is happy. As women, we can set a pleasant tone in the family and home with a calm, peaceful demeanor.

When you nurture peace in your heart, it will spill over onto your marriage, children and everyone you love. Don't worry. Pray. Rejoice. God's rules for peace – post them on the door to your heart.

Prayer: Dear Lord, I want a heart and home full of your indescribable peace. Help me to pray with a thankful heart and turn my worries over to you. In Jesus' name, Amen.

Banana Bread

Ingredients:

1 cup sugar
1 stick butter, softened
2 eggs
1/4 cup milk
1/2 teaspoon vinegar
1 teaspoon baking soda
1/3 cup sour cream
3 mashed really-ripe bananas
2 cups flour
1/2 cup chopped nuts (optional)

Directions:

Cream butter and sugar in large mixing bowl. Add eggs and blend well. In liquid measuring cup, mix milk, vinegar and baking soda. Stir until it foams slightly. Add to butter mixture, stir well and allow mixture to sit for 10 minutes. Add sour cream, bananas and nuts, if desired, and blend well. Stir in flour until just moistened. Pour into pan and bake as directed.

For 1 large loaf: 350 for 1 hour.
For 2 smaller loaves: 375 for 45 minutes
For ~15 muffins: 400 for 20 minutes

To make pumpkin bread, use a 15-ounce can of plain pumpkin instead of bananas and increase sugar to 1-1/4 cups.

#6
Divine Delays

We wait in hope for the Lord; he is our help and our shield.
Psalm 33:20

"Go night-night, Molly!" I said, trying to coax my miniature schnauzer into her crate so I could drive my son to school. She usually obeyed immediately, scooting inside and curling up in her soft afghan. But today she moseyed around the room sniffing the carpet then sat down and scratched behind her ear. As I shooed her in and closed the little door, a surprising thought interrupted my impatience: "I wonder if God is trying to delay us for some reason?"

On the way to school, I reflected on the likelihood of Molly's antics being a "divine delay." Perhaps God held us back long enough to miss a deer darting across the road. Maybe the holdup caused my son to connect with a particular classmate at they walked into school together. The possibilities were endless and gave me a new perspective about patience – a fruit of the spirit that doesn't come easily to many of us, especially me.

Don't you love being around patient people? I admire the way they bear setbacks and interruptions with a calm, unruffled demeanor and optimism. Today's verse might let us in on their secret to having patience while waiting – hope and prayer.

One way to cultivate patience is to be hopeful, instead of irritated, when you're delayed or waiting. We wait in hope for the Lord. Be open to the possibility that God may have orchestrated your holdup for a good reason. He may have a better plan that will bless you immensely, but requires your patience while circumstances come together.

In the Bible, Mary and Martha experienced a delay that threw them for a loop, but ended up being a blessing. Their brother Lazarus was gravely ill so they sent word to their good friend, Jesus, asking him to come. But Jesus purposely delayed his arrival by several days, and in the meantime Lazarus died and was buried.

When Jesus arrived, both sisters greeted Him with the same words: "Lord, if you would have been here, my brother would not have died." (John 11:21, 32b) Even through their grief, they showed faith that Jesus could have healed Lazarus. With Mary, Martha and a group of mourners as witnesses, Jesus went to the tomb. Jesus purposely made them wait because He wanted to perform an astonishing miracle to build everyone's faith. Instead of just healing his sickness, Jesus raised Lazarus from the dead. Wow!

Can you imagine the happy tears and joy shared at the tomb that day? Jesus turned mourning and waiting into gladness. God might make you wait for answers sometimes, too, and it's hard to be patient. Instead of getting frustrated or angry, remember to trust Him. When God allows a delay in your life, you can be confident that He has a good reason.

Another way to practice patience while waiting is to pray. The verse says God is our help and our shield. He's always there to help if we just ask. When you're waiting in line, instead of fretting about how long it's taking, say a prayer. In place of flipping through magazines in the dentist's waiting room, pray for your family members, one by one.

Waiting is part of life. We can be like the impatient child in the back seat asking "Are we there yet?" every five minutes. Or we can sit back and enjoy the ride, trusting that God's timing is best. Remember this rhyme for cultivating patience: If there's a delay, hope and pray!

Dear Lord, when I'm in a time of waiting, help me to place my hope and trust in your perfect timing. Allow me to practice patience by making waiting times into praying times. In Jesus' name, Amen.

Apricot Chicken

Ingredients:

4 boneless, skinless chicken breast halves, cut into
thin strips
1 green pepper, thinly sliced
1 tablespoon olive oil
1 teaspoon minced garlic
1/2 cup white cooking wine
1 tablespoon soy sauce
1/4 teaspoon ground ginger
1 tablespoon cornstarch
1 (15 ounce) can apricots including juice

Directions:

Drain apricots, reserving juice. In liquid measuring cup,
mix wine, 1/2 cup juice from apricots, soy sauce and ginger.
Set aside. Sauté chicken strips in olive oil until cooked, then
remove from pan. In same skillet, sauté green peppers and
garlic for about 2 minutes. Pour sauce mixture into skillet and
simmer for a few minutes. Add cornstarch to remaining apricot
juice and stir briskly. Add to sauce a little at a time, stirring
constantly, and cook until it thickens. Stir in chicken and
apricots. Makes 4 servings.

*Some apricot chicken recipes use jam, but whole apricots
add body and fiber. The sweetness of this dish goes well with
the nutty flavor of brown rice.*

#7
An Excuse to Be Kind

...and be kind to one another, tenderhearted,
forgiving one another, as God in Christ has forgiven you.
Ephesians 4:32

"Please, Mommy, let me take it to school for Emily," pleaded my eight-year-old son, as he cradled a fat, wriggly earthworm in his hands. Ben explained that his friend Emily had found an earthworm during recess, but when it accidentally got squished, she had cried.

I shook my head, rattling off all the reasons why it wasn't a good idea. Worms need to travel in dirt. Dirt could spill on the school bus. The teacher might not want dirt or a worm in the classroom.

"Please, Mommy," Ben pleaded, his eyes brimming with tears. "She was so sad and that made all the other girls in my class sad, too."

My heart almost burst. My sweet son wanted to take away his friend's sorrow and replace it with joy. Even though the idea sounded trivial to a grown-up, the small gesture of kindness was of grand importance to a child.

"Okay, you can give Emily the worm," I said. Kind gesture or not, I was wondering what Emily's mom, who was the school nurse, would think about Ben's gift.

As I watched him fill a plastic cup with dirt to make a worm house, I thanked God for giving Ben a kind heart. After all, God measures the value of a deed by the condition of the heart, not the greatness (or messiness) of the deed itself.

Kindness is one of the fruits of the spirit. Have you ever seen a stranger you knew was kindhearted, just by looking at her? Kindness produces an aura of softness, "smile crinkles" around the eyes and a glow to the complexion. A kind woman exudes the love of Jesus like a sweet fragrance and makes others feel warm and loved. Whether she is working on a project with a colleague or chatting with the grocery clerk, a kind woman gives thoughtful consideration to others.

For many women, performing kind deeds is often easier than acting cordial all the time or speaking in a civil tone under trying circumstances. Most of us truly want to be kind, but it's not always easy. It's tough to be pleasant when other people are rude or treat us unfairly. Sometimes it's hard to reach out to a complete stranger or even an acquaintance who rubs us the wrong way. And often we're feeling tired and rushed and just want to go home. But we're called to reflect the love of Jesus to those we come in contact with each day, whether we feel like it or not.

My pastor offered a technique to make kindness come more easily. It involves using your imagination to guess what is bothering irritable people. The next time you run into a difficult person, try making an excuse for her behavior. Maybe she's not feeling well. Maybe she got some bad news today. Maybe her earthworm got squished. Feeling empathy for a thorny person can soften our hearts and generate the compassion we need to offer a smile or a word of encouragement. Make an excuse, feel empathy, reach out with kindness – will you give it a try?

Prayer: Please help me to be kind and compassionate to others today. In Jesus' name, Amen.

Beth's Apple Muffins

Ingredients:

2 medium Granny Smith apples, peeled and finely
chopped
3/4 stick butter
1-1/3 cup sugar
1/2 cup applesauce
3/4 cup milk
1 egg
1 teaspoon vanilla
2 cups flour
1 teaspoon baking soda
2 teaspoons cinnamon

Directions:

Peel and chop apples and set aside. Place butter in glass
mixing bowl and melt in microwave. Stir in sugar, applesauce,
milk, egg and vanilla until well blended. Add dry ingredients
and mix until just combined. Fold in chopped apple. Fill
muffin papers or greased muffin cups 2/3 full. Bake at 400
degrees for about 20 minutes. Makes 16.

*Of all the muffins I make, my family likes these best. They
disappear fast!*

#8
Oh My Goodness!

How great is your goodness, which you have stored up for
those who fear you.
Psalm 31:19a

Goodness is a fruit of the spirit, but of all the character traits, it seems the hardest to define. The word "good" has been terribly over-used. We use it to exclaim surprise, as in "good grief!" or "oh my goodness!" We use it to describe good things – a good idea, a good day, a good friend. Sometimes we call bad things good – a good cigar, a good fight. With all this wishy-washiness, how are we to recognize authentic goodness when we see it?

In the Bible, the word "goodness" is most often used to describe God. Only God is truly "good," so all goodness comes directly from Him. During creation, God called everything he originally made "good." (Genesis 1:31a) Then Adam and Eve sinned in the garden, and humans haven't been innately good ever since. In fact, our natural inclination is to be...um, well, not good.

How can we get God's genuine goodness into ourselves? One way is to crack open our Bibles to read the stories and memorize verses. King David called it "hiding God's word in our hearts." As we read, we soak up God's wisdom into our hearts and minds. Then if difficult situations occur in daily life, we're equipped to discern the best things to say and do.

When we obey God and do what's right, His goodness and blessing flow through us. Being obedient means following God's precepts like telling the truth, showing compassion, practicing gratitude and doing excellent work. Doing the right thing, even when it's hard, is the goodness of God working through you.

Maintaining goodness is like keeping a closet clean. Both require daily upkeep or they get messy. I don't enjoy whipping a messy closet into shape, but I do it anyway - pull everything out, get rid of what we don't need and return the rest in a more orderly fashion. When I'm done, it feels great to have a tidy closet.

Happy to have things organized, I put things back where they belong for a while. Gloves in the basket on the floor. Coats on hangers. Flashlight on it's hook. That's good.

Then a jacket falls off the hanger. Gloves are tossed haphazardly, missing the basket. Gift bags fall out of their pocket organizer. Soon there's a pile of stuff on the floor that almost reaches the bottom of the coats. Disarray once again. Not good.

Sometimes I'm a mess, too. I neglect relationships. I complain too much. Usually those bad behaviors mean I've let a few days go by without soaking up God's word. It takes some effort to fix the messes I've made and whip myself into shape.

Whether it's trying to be good or trying to keep the closet neat, I have to work at it each day or things slip into disarray. Just like I was hesitant to clean the coat closet, I don't always feel like reading my Bible. Sometimes I would rather get busy on my to-do list for the day instead. But when I skip the reading, my "heart closet" gets jumbled and disordered, and I slip into sin. Cracking open the Bible each day replenishes my supply of God's goodness.

Next time you open a closet to hang up your coat, think about your Bible. Have you opened it today?

Prayer: Dear Lord, please give me the desire to read and memorize your Word so that your goodness can work through me. In Jesus' name, Amen.

Red Raspberry Smoothie

Ingredients:

1 cup red raspberries, fresh or frozen
1 large banana, sliced
1 cup vanilla yogurt
1/2 cup milk
1 teaspoon vanilla
2 teaspoons honey

Directions:

Place all ingredients in blender or food processor and blend until smooth. Makes 2 servings, 1-1/4 cup each.

This smoothie is a beautiful shade of pink and makes a delicious breakfast.

#9
Pears Stems and Coins

His master replied, "Well done, good and faithful servant!
You have been faithful with a few things; I will put you in
charge of many things."
Matthew 25:21a

Do you ever come home from the grocery store with fruit stems in your pockets? Sometimes I do, and they remind me of the fruit of the spirit called faithfulness.

One day, my younger son, Joey, was helping me choose fruit by packing pears in a produce bag. Last time, the sharp stems had torn through the plastic bag, causing pears to roll all over the conveyor belt at the checkout, so I asked Joey to break off the stems before bagging them. To demonstrate, I broke off a stem and dropped it back into the pear bin.

"Uh, Mom?" my older son, Ben said. "Should you put the stems back in with the pears? I bet Jesus would throw them in a trash can."

"But honey, there aren't any trash cans here," I said. "Lots of fruit stems and leaves collect in the bottom of the bins, so it's no big deal."

"Jesus would find a trash can," he said. I sighed, picturing myself stuffing pear stems into my jeans pockets and unloading them into the restroom trash can.

Pear stems are insignificant, yet figuring out how to dispose of them made me realize Ben was learning faithfulness – doing what God expects even in the smallest things.

In the parable of the talents in Matthew 25, the master tests the faithfulness of his servants. He gives responsibilities to three of them based on their abilities. Before going out of town, the master gives five coins to one servant, two coins to another and one coin to another. The first two servants used the money wisely and doubled the investments for their master. But the last servant dug a hole and hid the money, so it gained nothing.

The master praised the first two servants for their faithfulness in small things. In fact, the servants' performances in this small matter were used to decide how much additional responsibility they would be given. The first two passed the test and were promoted. The unfaithful servant was kicked out of the household.

Faithfulness is both believing and doing. First, the servants believed in their master. They trusted he would come home and reward them. Second, they did something for the master by taking care of his business, the coins. Believing + doing = faithfulness.

How can we be like the faithful servants? We can believe in God and do something for Him. We can faithfully use whatever "coins" God has given us, whether it is many coins or just a select few.

"Coins" are any responsibilities, talents or material things God has given us, not just money. Maybe you have big responsibilities like being a nurse or counselor. Perhaps you have talents like a beautiful singing voice or a knack for gardening. You have a certain amount of income. All of these things are your "coins." How you use your coins is the measure of your faithfulness.

One of my husband's coins is teaching the adult Sunday school class at our church. To remind him of the weighty responsibility of this and other tasks, he keeps this verse on his desk: "To whom much is given, much is expected." (Luke 12:48.) The more coins you have, the more faithful you can be.

Take inventory of your coins – your responsibilities, talents and material blessings. Which one will you use today to show your faithfulness?

Prayer: Lord, thank you for the coins you have provided in my life. Remind me to be faithful in using them to serve so that someday I will hear you say, "Well done, good and faithful servant." In Jesus' name, Amen.

Spiced Pear Butter

Ingredients:

6 pears, peeled and coarsely chopped
1/3 cup orange juice
1/3 cup brown sugar
1/2 teaspoon cinnamon
dash of ginger

Directions:

In saucepan, simmer pears and orange juice over medium heat. Stir frequently, replacing lid to keep moisture inside. Add brown sugar, cinnamon and ginger and continue cooking until pears are soft. Pour into food processor and blend until smooth. Makes 2 cups.

Makes a sweet, smooth topping for oatmeal, toast, pancakes, waffles, yogurt or ice cream.

#10
Pop Goes the Diva

A gentle answer turns away wrath, but a harsh word stirs up anger.
Proverbs 15:1

There's nothing like the sweet-and-tart flavor of freshly made cranberry sauce to go with turkey and stuffing. But cranberry sauce isn't just for Thanksgiving. I make it year-round from the supply of berries I stash in the freezer each fall.

Cranberries simmering on the stove leave a sweet aroma in the air. The pleasant fragrance lingers even after the cranberry sauce is gone. Do you leave a sweet scent behind? I don't mean your perfume or mouthwash. I'm talking about the fruit of the spirit called gentleness. Gentle women have a soothing effect on others, making the atmosphere around them seem calm and unhurried – almost sweet.

Homemade cranberry sauce is sweet, but it doesn't start out that way. If you've ever bitten into a raw cranberry, you know they are pucker-your-lips tart. The funny thing is, in order to transform into sweet sauce, each berry has to explode. If you listen closely when the berries are simmering, you will hear the gentle "pop" as the skin bursts open. Popping allows the tangy insides to blend with the sugary cooking liquid. Popping open and spilling its guts is the first step toward a cranberry becoming sweeter.

Like cranberries on their way to becoming sauce, I've had to "pop" a few times on my way to becoming sweeter. I get angry, say things that aren't very nice and then feel guilty about it. Angry words rarely help anything, but gentle words soothe hurts, build others up and make them feel loved. I need to work on answering gently, even when I'm angry and feel like bursting instead.

Have you ever exploded in anger, then felt ashamed about your outburst? Seeing our own capability to spew bitterness can cause us to take a hard look at ourselves. Sometimes a big "pop" makes us aware of our own sour attitudes. Popping can be the beginning of a sweetening process as we make efforts to be more calm and gentle.

Remember Mary and Martha, the sisters who were good friends of Jesus? When Jesus was visiting them, Mary was hanging with Jesus, leaving Martha alone in the kitchen. Martha said, "Lord, don't you care that my sister has left me to do the work by myself? Tell her to help me!" Notice the exclamation point? It signifies that Martha is popping, spewing out the sour stuff inside her heart.

Jesus tried to calm Martha down with gentle words. "Martha, Martha," the Lord answered, "You are worried and upset about many things, but only one thing is needed. Mary has chosen what is better, and it will not be taken away from her." (Luke 10:40-41)

I love that Jesus said "Martha, Martha." He repeated her name as if trying to get her attention and ease her irritation. I imagine he looked into her eyes and spoke quietly, even though his words were firm. The Bible doesn't describe Martha's response to Jesus, but I suspect her annoyance melted away at his soothing words. A gentle answer turns away wrath.

As we cultivate gentleness, we must be careful not to mistake it for weakness. Gentle women are not doormats. In fact, gentleness is actually strength in disguise. It takes a strong woman to hold herself in check and treat others with tenderness. So the goal is to keep your spunk, but be gentle.

After cranberry sauce is cooked, it's still a bit tangy, yet tempered by an overwhelming sweetness. I want to be like that – a woman with a unique personality softened with gentleness, who leaves others with a sweet feeling.

Prayer: Dear Lord, give me the strength to be gentle even when I feel like "popping." In Jesus' name, Amen.

Cherry Cranberry Sauce

Ingredients:

1 bag (12 ounces) whole cranberries
1 cup cherry juice
1 cup sugar
1/4 teaspoon cinnamon
1-1/2 cups sweet cherries, pitted and halved (fresh,
canned or frozen)

Directions:

If using frozen cherries, thaw to room temperature. In a
medium saucepan over high heat, bring juice and sugar to a
boil. Add cinnamon and cranberries. Reduce heat to medium
and boil gently for about five minutes, stirring occasionally,
until all cranberries have popped. Don't overcook or
cranberries may become bitter. Remove from heat and stir in
sweet cherries. Cool to room temperature. Store in refrigerator.
Makes about 3 cups.

*Cranberries may protect against some kinds of cancers,
heart disease and stomach ulcers. Antioxidants called
proanthocyanidins in cranberries fight urinary tract infections
by preventing bacteria from sticking to the bladder walls.*

#11
Sweet Temptations

*Like a city whose walls are broken down is a man who lacks
self-control.*
Proverbs 25:28

When it comes to chocolate candy, I'm like a city with broken down walls. I have no defenses. If there is chocolate in my house, I will be tempted over and over until I give in and eat it, lots of it. I guess that's the definition of a chocoholic. We laugh about it, but it's really not funny. Giving in to temptation is a lack of self-control, plain and simple. Each time I give in to eating more chocolate, "city walls" of my health break down even more, leaving me vulnerable to even more destruction. As everyone in my family knows, I need more self-control when it comes to chocolate.

Self-control is one of the fruits of the spirit. The term "self-control" is a bit misleading and is often confused with "willpower." It suggests that we can stop ourselves from doing the very thing we want to avoid, whether it's gossiping, overindulging in chocolate or flirting with a colleague at work. Willing ourselves to stop doing these things may not work because our human weakness is no match for temptation. Oftentimes we give in to the self-indulgent behavior and end up feeling empty and alone.

Thankfully, there is no need to fight temptation alone! Believe it or not, real self-control happens when we relinquish control to someone else, someone stronger. When we turn our wills and hearts over to God, He becomes our partner in self-control. God provides the supernatural strength to defend against temptations we can't resist on our own.

Think about a specific situation where temptation causes you to lose control. As an example, let's say you and your coworkers chitchat in a faultfinding manner about others at lunchtime. To practice self-control in this situation, try these five steps:

1. Identify the temptation; (Gossiping with coworkers at lunch.)

2. Pray about it, confessing your sin and asking for strength; (Dear Lord, I am a gossip and it is wrong. Please help me to overcome the temptation to be critical and spread rumors.)

3. List the benefits of self-control; (I would feel better about myself and improve my reputation. I could set a godly example for my coworkers.)

4. Make a plan to prevent the temptation from reoccurring;. (Decide ahead of time that you won't add to the gossip discussion.)

5. Substitute something good. (Remain silent during the tittle-tattle discussions. Say complimentary things about others instead.)

You can apply these steps to any circumstances. For my sweet temptation, my plan in step 4 is to stop putting mini chocolate bars in my shopping cart. For step 5, I can eat a banana with a thin coating of antioxidant-rich dark chocolate instead.

Is cultivating self-control easy? Nope. But it's a daily battle that is worth fighting. Don't let your city walls fall down around you by struggling alone. God is waiting for you to ask for help in whatever temptation you are facing today.

Prayer: Dear Lord, I don't want to go it alone against the temptations in my life. Please provide your supernatural strength to help me stand strong against things that entice me. In Jesus' name, Amen.

Frozen Chocolate-Covered Bananas

Ingredients:

1/2 cup semi-sweet chocolate chips
1/2 teaspoon vegetable oil
2 medium bananas
4 wooden sticks

Directions:

Melt chocolate chips in glass dish in microwave 30 seconds at a time, stirring in between. When chips are almost melted, add oil and stir well. Peel bananas, cut in half crosswise and insert wooden sticks into cut edges. Dip bananas in melted chocolate, using spoon to coat entire banana half and scrape off excess. Place on wax paper-lined baking sheet and put in freezer for several hours. Enjoy!

This is a fun-to-eat chocolate treat you can feel good about eating and serving to your family. The thin coating of chocolate satisfies a craving while the banana provides fiber and heart-healthy potassium.

#12
Medicinal Fruit

Then God said, "I give you every seed-bearing plant...and every tree that has fruit with seed in it. They will be yours for food."
Genesis 1:29

There are zillions of reasons why I love fruit. It's pretty. It tastes sweet and smells nice. It's a quick, easy snack. Most importantly, it's natural, without the synthetic junk found in processed foods.

Fruit is natural because God made it. In fact, fruits were probably the first foods Adam and Eve ate. I'm pretty sure the Garden of Eden didn't have donut trees or French fry trees. While the world was still perfect, God provided fruit as food. That gives me total confidence in its nutritional value.

Modern science confirms that God loaded fruits with substances that promote health – fiber, minerals, vitamins and antioxidants. Antioxidants are plant compounds that defend healthy tissue from free radicals. Think of free radicals as bad guys that can damage our cells at the molecular level and cause disease. One way antioxidants protect us is by neutralizing those tiny bad guys so they can't hurt us. Studies show that a diet rich in fruits, vegetables and whole grains – foods high in antioxidants – can help reduce the risk of many diseases.

As a dietitian, I love to learn about the different antioxidants. Some vitamins function as antioxidants, like vitamin C and A. Vitamin C is found in strawberries and citrus fruits like oranges and limes. Vitamin A and antioxidants called carotenoids are found in apricots, peaches and cantaloupe. Cranberries and purple grapes contain flavonoids. Lycopene is found in watermelon and pink grapefruit. These are just a few examples. Scientists continue to learn more about antioxidants and how they work together in the body. Nutrition experts tell us to eat a "variety of foods" because that's an easy way to get as assortment of antioxidants each day.

I want my family to be healthy so I feed them lots of fruit. My two sons, now teenagers, are used to me asking, "How many servings of fruit have you had today?" They choose their own breakfast each morning, but I usually set fruit at their places before they come to the kitchen – a banana, a bowl of berries, sometimes fruit salad. I pack fruit in lunch boxes every day for the boys and for my husband. Eating fruit at every meal provides a constant supply of antioxidants for their bodies.

Fruits of the spirit characteristics are like "antioxidants for the soul." Each character trait builds our spiritual health to help fight against different kinds of sin. For example, cultivating joy helps protect us from murmuring and complaining. Cultivating gentleness helps guard against harsh words. Just like fruit helps keep our bodies strong, fruits of the spirit improve our spiritual health.

When we exhibit patience or goodness, it is like medicine for the hearts and souls of others, too. Think of all the ways you could help someone else by demonstrating a fruit of the spirit.

You could:

-Soothe an aching heart with kindness and love.
-Prevent hurt feelings by exercising self-control.
-Erase fear with your example of peace and gentleness.
-Replace hopelessness by sharing your joy.
-Drive out mistrust with a display of faithfulness.

When fruit-of-the-spirit traits become part of your personality, you minister to the hearts and souls of other people each day, often without even realizing it!

Edible fruit promotes physical health. Fruits of the spirit promote spiritual health and bless others at the same time. How much fruit have YOU had today?

Prayer: Dear Lord, thank you for all I'm learning about edible fruit and fruits of the spirit. Help me to utilize both kinds of fruit to keep me healthy, both physically and spiritually. In Jesus' name, Amen.

Cranberry Apple Bake

Ingredients:

5-6 large apples, peeled and thinly sliced
1-1/2 cups fresh cranberries
1/4 cup sugar
1/2 cup brown sugar
3 tablespoons flour
1/2 teaspoon cinnamon
1/4 teaspoon allspice
1/2 cup milk

Directions:

Mix sugars, flour and spices in a small bowl and set aside. Place apple slices and cranberries in a large bowl and sprinkle with sugar and spice mixture. Stir to coat. Dump fruit into greased 3-quart casserole dish. Drizzle with milk. Bake uncovered at 350 degrees for 1 hour or until apples are soft, stirring every 20 minutes. Makes 5-6 servings.

A perfect blend of sweet and tart, this dish is like apple pie without the high-fat crust. Fresh cranberries are in season from September through December. Stock your freezer with extra bags to use all year.

#13
Bearing Fruit

This is to my Father's glory, that you bear much fruit,
showing yourselves to be my disciples.
John 15:8

According to today's verse, bearing fruit demonstrates to the world that you are a disciple of Jesus. Whereas fruit-of-the-spirit traits like perseverance and self-control are internal fruit, bearing fruit is external fruit. Just as certain trees and bushes produce fruit, people can bear fruit, too.

In his book Secrets of the Vine, author Bruce Wilkinson says this about bearing fruit: "In practical terms, fruit represents good works – a thought, attitude, or action of ours that God values because it glorifies Him." Put another way, it means bearing fruit is anything you do, say or think that brings glory to God.

Conversely, anything we do, say or think that does not bring glory to God is not bearing fruit. It's important that our good works are actual fruit, not just nice things we do that don't glorify God. How do we make sure our good works bring glory to God?

I believe there are two things that transform ordinary actions into "bearing fruit" – the right attitude and giving credit for the deed to God.

Cultivating a joyful attitude about serving others is the first step towards bearing fruit. When we do things solely to show our love for God and our gratefulness for His blessings, that's the right attitude. That mindset allows us to honor and worship God.

On the other hand, grumbling keeps the focus on ourselves. If I mutter about how no one helps me around the house as I drag a trash bag out the back door, it turns my act of service into rotten fruit. When the chore is done with a bad attitude, it's like offering God a bruised, wormy apple. If my goal is to demonstrate my love and gratitude to God, nothing but praise could possibly flow from my lips.

The second step to fruit-bearing is to acknowledge God. Recognizing God's role in the activity doesn't have to be said out loud or made into a big fuss. Just silently thanking Him for allowing you to help someone is enough. It's easy to feel puffed up and proud when we do good works. Remembering that every talent, skill and dollar we have comes from God keeps us humble and grateful for the opportunity to use those resources in His name.

When you receive accolades on a good deed, that's an opening to give God the applause. Let's say someone compliments you on the pretty baby blankets you knitted for a local women's shelter. If you simply thank the person, it elevates only you. Giving God credit sounds more like this: "You know, God gave me the knack for knitting, so it's my privilege to use it for the babies." Acknowledging God's provision of your kitting talent turns those baby blankets into fruit.

I wonder how many plain old good deeds I've done when I could have been bearing fruit as an offering to my Lord? I don't want to waste another minute being less fruitful than God designed me to be. First, I will cultivate an attitude of gladness, reminding myself that no matter what the task, I will do it with a joyful heart as an act of worship. Second, I will uncover opportunities to give credit to God for every act of service He allows me to do.

If you're like most women, you do nice things for others all the time. Starting today, will you begin transforming your good deeds into bearing fruit?

Prayer: Dear Lord, I want to bear fruit that points others to you. As I serve, give me a joyful heart and occasions to acknowledge you as the source of every good thing. In Jesus' name, Amen.

Homemade Chewy Granola Bars

Ingredients:

3 cups quick oats
2 tablespoons melted butter
2 tablespoons honey
1 can (14 ounces) sweetened condensed milk
2 cups dried cranberries
1 cup miniature chocolate chips
1/2 cup chopped nuts

Directions:

Place oats in large mixing bowl. Melt butter in small bowl in microwave then stir in honey. Drizzle over oats and stir well. Pour condensed milk over oats and stir again. Add dried cranberries, chocolate chips and nuts and stir everything together until well-blended.

Spread in greased 9x13 inch pan and pat down. Bake at 350 degrees about 20 minutes or until edges turn slightly brown. Cool for a few minutes, then cut into 21 servings (3 rows of 7 rectangles each.)

Great for breakfast on-the-go or as a lunchbox treat. You can switch out the cranberries for other kinds of dried fruit to suit your family's tastes.

#14
Yucky Grapes

"My grace is sufficient for you, for power is made perfect in weakness."
2 Corinthians 12:9a

My four-year-old son appeared to be playing with his snack, a bunch of grapes. He popped one grape in his mouth, then placed two on his napkin. Curious, I asked Joey why he was putting some of the grapes aside.

"These grapes are yucky," he announced, pointing to the pile on the napkin.

"What's wrong with them?" I asked.

"They have ouchies," he said. Joey pointed to a squishy brown spot where one grape was attached to the stem, small puckers in another grape's skin and other minor cosmetic imperfections.

"It's okay to eat the ouchie grapes," I advised. "They taste good."

Joey crinkled his nose and shook his head. "No, thanks, I don't want them."

Perhaps you can empathize because one of your children is a fussy eater or has quirks about what kinds of foods are truly edible. Obviously, no mom wants to serve rotten food to her family, but grapes with "ouchies" are natural. The fruit still tastes fine and provides good nutrition.

In today's world, children learn at a young age that "spots" or imperfections are undesirable. Our society seems to prize air-brushed beauty, perfectly toned bodies and vivacious personalities. Having any kind of personal imperfection or weakness is seen as a bad thing.

No matter how old we are, we tend to compare ourselves to others. We criticize each other's "ouchies" and make judgments about each other's character. We arrange people into categories in our minds just like Joey sorted his grapes into piles. These people are my friends. These people are too grouchy. These people are too controlling. And on and on we classify others based on our assessment. But at the same time, we hope others overlook our faults!

The apostle Paul from the Bible viewed flaws in a different light. He said our weaknesses have the potential to make us strong. That doesn't seem to make sense at first, because flaws make us feel incapable or inferior, not strong.

It's the hidden opportunity in weakness that Paul wants us to understand. When we feel inadequate, we're more likely to rely on God for strength. Weakness can draw us closer to the Lord as we seek His direction for accomplishing daunting tasks or dealing with difficult people.

Instead of focusing on our many flaws, God views each of us as a "work in progress." He knows we're not perfect. But unlike bruised fruit, which can't be fixed, we can change our thinking and gain insights into how to do things differently.

When we go to the Lord in prayer, He gently points out the places we need guidance. When we cry out for help, He provides strength. God infuses His power into weak, imperfect people who are willing to humble themselves and submit to His leading.

Thank goodness we serve a God who isn't as picky about His servants as Joey was about his grapes. When God sees an imperfection, He doesn't pluck us from the vine and call us yucky. Instead He actually chooses women like us, despite our spots and puckers, as workers in His earthly vineyard.

Prayer: Lord, help me to immediately look to You for guidance when I feel inadequate. In Jesus' name, Amen.

Fruity Chicken Salad

Ingredients:

4 cooked chicken breast halves, cubed
2 cups seedless green grapes, halved lengthwise
2/3 cup cherry-flavored dried cranberries
1 cup pineapple tidbits, drained

Dressing:
1/2 cup sour cream
1/4 cup honey
Dash of ground ginger (optional)

Directions:

Combine chicken and fruit in medium bowl. Whisk dressing ingredients in a liquid measuring cup until blended. Pour over chicken and fruit and stir to coat. Makes about 6 servings.

This recipe is perfect when you're having a friend or two over for lunch. Serve chicken salad on a bed of baby spinach and bitter greens. Add a basket of corn muffins and a pitcher of iced tea and you're good to go.

#15
Fruit with a Purpose

*For we are God's workmanship, created in Christ Jesus to
do good works, which God prepared in advance for us to do.*
Ephesians 2:10

God knows everything. He knows how many honeybees
pollinate each cherry blossom. He knows how many peaches,
oranges or apricots each tree will produce. While it's still on
the tree, God knows whether each individual fruit will be made
into juice, jam or wine or whether it will be frozen or canned.
He even knows who will eventually eat each piece of fruit.

If God knows every detail about ordinary fruit, surely He
knows about you! Human beings are the pièce de résistance
or the "main event" of creation. Not only does He count the
hairs on your head, but He has a plan for your life, including
how you will bear fruit. Today's verse declares that when God
was creating you, He already planned out opportunities for you
to do good works. There are divinely-designated projects out
there with your name on them! Isn't that incredible?

You may be wondering how to decide what fruit-bearing
activities to try. There are entire books written about spiritual
gifts and how to discover your niche for serving others. Or you
can follow these three simple steps:

First, make a list of things you love to do. Take a few days
to think about it and keep adding to the list as things come to
mind. Don't discount anything as silly or frivolous. If you like
to paint ceramics, wax the car or alphabetize your books, add

it to the list. God can help you find an outlet for any aptitude He has given you.

Second, armed with your list, spend some time alone with God asking him to show you his plans. A suitable scripture to focus on is Matthew 5:16: "...let your light shine before men, that they may see your good deeds and praise your father in heaven." Since you are his workmanship, God is willing to reveal the tasks he has bookmarked for you.

Third, make an effort to serve others through items on your list that God has underscored during your prayer time. For example, if you love to cook, try volunteering at a soup kitchen or Meals on Wheels. Or whip up a meal for a new mom or someone who is recuperating from surgery.

Pray that God would give you contentment as a clear confirmation of which fruit-bearing tasks he wants you to undertake and continue. Some opportunities will be brief encounters as you go about your day, like being kind to a stressed-out waitress. Other times God may offer you a longer assignment, like supporting a friend through cancer treatment. Maybe you will bear fruit via a lifetime appointment, like adopting a child.

Remember, what the world thinks of your "fruit" isn't what matters. What counts is fulfilling the plans God has for you. When your good works match up with God's blueprint, you'll be bearing your own unique fruit. How sweet is that?

Prayer: Dear Lord, I want to accomplish the good works you planned for me. Please show me how to bear fruit according to your design in every situation. In Jesus' name, Amen.

Cranberry Rice Pilaf

Ingredients:

3 tablespoons extra-virgin olive oil
2 large red onions, chopped
1-1/2 teaspoons cinnamon
1/2 cup water
1/2 cup dried cranberries
One 14-ounce box minute rice

Directions:

Cook rice on stovetop or microwave according to package directions. Meanwhile, sauté onion in olive oil over medium heat until soft. Sprinkle cinnamon over onions and stir until well blended. Add water and cranberries and simmer for about 5 minutes, stirring frequently. Add cranberry mixture to hot rice and stir well. Makes 8 servings.

This is a healthy alternative to flavored rice mixes, which are loaded with sodium and additives. Using brown minute rice gives the dish a slightly nutty flavor and lots more fiber.

#16
Apple of God's Eye

*Keep me as the apple of your eye; hide me in the shadow of
your wings*
Psalm 17:8

Tamara sunk into the couch, exhausted from a long day at the office. Before she could go to bed, there were mounds of laundry to tackle and dinner to cook. The door flew open and her teenage daughter stormed through the living room, without even a glance in her mother's direction, and stomped up the stairs to her room. Tamara's husband followed, mumbling under his breath and asking if supper was ready.

Sighing softly, Tamara plucked a daisy from a vase on the coffee table. "He loves me, he loves me not..." she said, tearing off petals one by one. Instead of being queen of her invincible castle, she felt like the maid in a falling-down fortress with no knight in shining armor in sight.

Do you ever feel invisible instead of like a well-loved wife and mother? Husbands can be uncommunicative or demanding. Small children require constant attention, teens can be rebellious and adult children may not call often. There may be days when you wonder, "Does anyone love me?"

Take heart, dear sister, for you are cherished by your Father in heaven. He sees you as a treasure of immeasurable worth. How do I know God loves you? Because He tells us over and over in the Bible. "I have loved you with an everlasting love; I have drawn you with loving-kindness." (Jeremiah 31:3b) An everlasting love is forever. God will always love you and draw you to Himself.

No matter where you are or what you are doing, God loves you and cares for you. He loves you if you're flying in an airplane or scrubbing your bathtub. He loves you if you're driving in a snowstorm, sitting in a movie theater or asleep in your bed. He loves you across time – when you were a baby, teenager and now. He loves you every single millisecond of your life.

God loves you so much that nothing can separate you from His love. Absolutely nothing. The Bible says "...neither death nor life, neither angels nor demons, neither the present nor the future, nor any powers, neither height nor depth, nor anything else in all creation, will be able to separate us from the love of God that is in Christ Jesus our Lord." (Romans 8:38-39)

The most awesome expression of God's love is that He sent Jesus down to earth. "For God so loved the world that he gave his one and only Son, that whoever believes in him shall not perish but have eternal life." (John 3:16) God could have made us work for our salvation, but He didn't. It's a free gift. All we have to do is believe that Jesus died for our sins and ask Him to be our Lord and Savior. Then He reserves a place for us in heaven. That's true love.

God holds us close, whether we can feel it or not. "He tends his flock like a shepherd: He gathers the lambs in his arms and carries them close to his heart..." (Isaiah 41:11a)

Close your eyes. Imagine God holding you on his lap in a warm, comforting embrace. Ask Him to encircle you with a tangible sense of His presence. Whether you're a wife, mother, daughter, sister or grandmother, sink this truth deep into your heart: the Creator of the universe adores you. You're the apple of God's eye!

Prayer: Thank you for loving me unconditionally Lord, no matter where I am, what I'm doing or how I feel. Please help me to accept your love and share it with those around me. In Jesus' name, Amen.

Apple French Toast Casserole

Ingredients:

1/2 cup butter
3/4 cup packed brown sugar
2 tablespoons honey
3 large tart apples, peeled and sliced 1/4-inch thick
cinnamon
3 eggs
1 cup milk
1 teaspoon vanilla
8 slices day-old French bread (3/4-inch thick)

Directions:

In small saucepan, melt butter then stir in brown sugar and honey. Heat on low for 2-3 minutes until thick. Pour into ungreased 13x9 baking dish. Arrange apples on top of syrup in 1-2 layers. Sprinkle lightly with cinnamon. Beat eggs, milk and vanilla in bowl. Dip bread into mixture, turning to coat. Place bread on top of apples. Cover and refrigerate overnight. Remove from fridge 30 minutes before baking. Bake uncovered at 350 for 35-40 minutes. Serve warm.

Great recipe when you have overnight guests. Make it the night before and have breakfast in a jiffy.

#17
Cherry Pie Treasures

But store up for yourselves treasures in heaven...
for where your treasure is, there your heart will be also.
Matthew 6:20a-21

For about ten years we had a sour cherry tree in our back yard. Every summer we picked the cherries and froze them. During the winter, I made pies from our cherry stash.

Sounds fun, doesn't it? In reality, getting the cherries from the tree to the freezer was a ton of work. There were three steps before the cherries were ready to use - picking, pitting and packaging.

We watched closely for the cherries to begin ripening. At the first glimpse of red on the edge of the fruit, we hung aluminum pie tins amongst the tree branches to scare away feathered cherry thieves – blackbirds. When the cherries were fully ripe, we hauled buckets and a step ladder outside. As the boys grew, picking became a family affair, with them in charge of the lower branches.

Next, I spent hours standing at the kitchen sink removing the pits. To package them, I scooped four cups of pitted cherries, enough for one pie, into each zippered freezer bag.

Pitting by hand seemed to take forever, so I monitored my progress and cheered myself on. "Two bags ready-to-freeze already – yay!" "Keep going. Think how yummy the pies will taste at Christmas." "Wow, eight bags done - think how many pies you can make for friends." Later, as I stashed the fruits of my labor in the freezer, having stained fingernails for the next few days seemed a small price to pay.

We didn't mind picking, pitting and packaging in July to reap the benefits in February. It was heavenly to thaw a bag of cherries in wintertime and bake up the taste of summer. A slice of pie made from real sour cherries is truly a treasure.

Pie is tasty, but the best treasures are the ones we store up for ourselves in heaven. How exactly do we do that? I think the answer lies in the first four verses of Matthew 6. The verses caution us against seeking man's accolades for doing good works. The verses say that when we make a big deal about our good deeds so that other people know, their praise is the only reward we will receive. Instead, whenever possible we should do good works quietly and humbly, so that only God sees. That's when God rewards us with treasure stored in heaven.

If I give a cherry pie to a friend's family and tell them how I picked and pitted the cherries myself, their appreciation is my only reward. But when I quietly donate a homemade cherry pie to a soup kitchen, God rewards me with treasure in heaven.

You'll be surprised at how much joy wells up inside you from secretly doing a kind deed. It's so exciting sharing a secret with God! You are doubly blessed - storing up treasures in heaven while having fun on earth at the same time.

What will our treasures in heaven be like? I don't know. But anything given to us by God will be absolutely wonderful, that's for sure.

Prayer: Dear Lord, I yearn for your approval and your reward for my good deeds. Help me to find opportunities to serve others in secret, so my treasures will accrue in heaven, not on earth. In Jesus' name, Amen.

Sour Cherry Cobbler

Ingredients:

2 cups sour cherries
1/2 cup sugar
2 tablespoons flour
1/2 cup butter
1 cup sugar
2 eggs
1/2 teaspoon vanilla
2/3 cup milk
2 teaspoons lemon juice
2 cups flour
1 tablespoon baking powder

Directions:

In a medium bowl, mix cherries with 1/2 cup sugar and 2 tablespoons flour and set aside. In a large bowl, cream butter, sugar, eggs and vanilla. Stir lemon juice into milk and blend into butter mixture. Mix in dry ingredients. Spread half of batter in greased 13 X 9 inch baking dish. Spoon cherry mixture evenly over top, then cover with rest of batter. Bake at 350 degrees for 40-45 minutes.

To substitute raspberries or blueberries, just decrease the sugar you mix with berries to 1/4 cup.

#18
Grapefruit Juice in Your Eye

Nobody should seek his own good, but the good of others.
I Corinthians 10:24

My grandmother ate half of a grapefruit every morning for breakfast. When I was a kid, we would sit in her breakfast nook digging out grapefruit sections with special spoons. The spoon tip was zigzagged with little metal teeth that pierced the membranes so you could scoop out the fruit. The only problem was, each time you pushed the spoon in, juice squirted out. Eating grapefruit is a good thing, but a spray of sour juice in your eye stings!

Have you ever tried to do something good and you end up getting a squirt of sour words? Sometimes the very person you are trying to help can get offended instead of being grateful.

When I see someone in the grocery store riding a scooter, I often offer to help them reach something on the top shelf. Most folks are appreciative. One time a scooter rider was behind me in the checkout line, so I offered to help put her groceries on the belt. She looked up at me and snarled "I can take care of myself!" I backed away, shocked by her acidic reaction.

Well, fine! I thought, wiping the imaginary grapefruit juice out of my eye. God quickly softened my heart and I realized that someone who reacts that way must be hurting. Perhaps she was frustrated about her loss of mobility and independence. Maybe she didn't feel well. Whatever her reasons for being short with me, she did a great job of putting everything on the belt by herself.

Even the good deeds Jesus did were not met with gladness by all who witnessed them. When Jesus healed the blind and sick, the religious leaders often criticized him instead of praising God and being joyful for the healed person. Can you imagine healing someone, only to have onlookers criticize you and plot to kill you? Talk about grapefruit juice in your eye! Since Jesus himself received that kind of treatment for performing miracles, it's not surprising that our humble attempts at offering aid might be rebuffed.

Did Jesus get offended by the religious leaders' condemnation of his good works and stop doing good things? Nope. He kept on offering compassion, kindness and assistance to people everywhere he went.

Jesus supernaturally knew the desires of each person's heart, but we won't know unless we ask. In our eagerness to rally to someone's aid, sometimes we make faulty assumptions about the best way to meet their needs. Just because you would want a certain kind of help in a particular situation doesn't mean others will. When we give the wrong kind of help, that's when people get offended and the grapefruit juice squirts back at us.

God loves it when you help others, so don't give up. If someone resists your help or is offended by an offer of charity, try to put yourself in her shoes. Allow God to fill your heart with compassion and show sensitivity to her feelings. Sometimes a tactfully phrased question geared to the situation will help you assess her mindset and discern what actions will be truly helpful. Better yet, just ask: "What can I do that would be the most helpful to you?"

Prayer: Dear Lord, sometimes my best intentions for doing good turn sour. Help me to be sensitive and compassionate so I can offer the right kind of help at just the right time. In Jesus' name, Amen.

Grapefruit & Mango Salad

Ingredients:

1 head Romaine lettuce, torn into pieces
1/2 small red onion, sliced
1 sectioned pink grapefruit with sections cut in half crosswise
2 mangos, diced
1/2 cup shredded cheddar cheese

Dressing:
1/4 cup balsamic vinegar
1/3 cup extra virgin olive oil
1/2 teaspoon ground ginger
1/4 teaspoon cumin
3/4 teaspoon salt
3 tablespoons sugar

Directions

Mix lettuce, onion, grapefruit and mango in large bowl. Sprinkle with cheddar cheese. Drizzle with dressing and toss to coat or serve dressing on side. Serve immediately.

Tart grapefruit, sweet mango, crisp lettuce plus a dash of ginger make this salad an amazing blend of textures and flavors.

#19
The Grapes of Wrath

Everyone should be quick to listen, slow to speak and slow to become angry.
James 1:19b

Think about the last time you got angry. How did you respond? Did you yell? Stew about it for hours or days? Give someone the silent treatment? Did you rehearse the unpleasant incident over and over in your mind until your stomach was in knots?

Everyone gets angry from time to time. Anger is not a sin. But the way we choose to respond to it can hurt ourselves and others. Just like fruit bruises when it's bumped around, people bruise easily when treated harshly. How can we deal with anger in a way that pleases God and doesn't hurt others?

When I think of anger, a Veggie Tales® story comes to mind. It's about a family of sour grapes who call themselves "The Grapes of Wrath." Ma and Pa Grape and their kids are a grumpy, argumentative bunch who fuss and fume at each other and others. When they meet Junior Asparagus, the grape kids ridicule him by making fun of his hair and calling him names. Seeing the grapes bully his son makes Junior's dad angry, but he handles the situation wisely. He doesn't shout or call the grapes names in return. Instead he patiently, but pointedly, explains to the grapes that their actions hurt Junior's feelings and make God sad. As a result, the grape family vows to put aside their grumbling and bullying and focus on being sweeter.

This story is geared toward children, but in our discontented society, adults can be "angry grapes," too. Some people go through life at a simmer, with resentment fermenting just below the surface. They bristle when anyone disagrees with their opinions. It takes only a minor conflict to make them blow up, spewing unpleasantness on those around them. Do you know anyone who behaves like that?

Name-calling isn't just a kid thing either. Adults do it in television shows and movies. Comedians use verbal put-downs of themselves and others in their acts – and people actually think it's funny. It's hard to find a comedian telling good, clean jokes without verbal bullying. Recent years have shown the advent of cyberspace anger where people "flame" each other by typing nasty comments on social network sites.

Then there's road rage where feuding drivers may actually harm one another. Have you ever gotten irritated while driving? "Did you see that guy cut me off? What an idiot!" I'm guilty. When another driver does something foolish or risky that puts my family in jeopardy, it raises my ire.

There will always be people or situations in life that annoy us or make us hopping mad. The question is, how will we handle those feelings? We can allow ourselves to be enslaved by anger, rehashing offenses until it affects our physical and mental health. Or we can respond in a godly fashion, like Junior's dad in the Grapes of Wrath story.

When anger knocks on the door to our hearts, we can do two simple steps - pause and pray:

PAUSE. Stop what you're doing for a minute. Try to pinpoint precisely what is ruffling your feathers. Sometimes taking a deep, cleansing breath helps. Walking away to think about the situation helps diffuse irritated emotions.

PRAY. Tell God what's going on. "I am so ticked off right now because..." Don't worry about God being offended. He already knows all about it. Ask God to help you put aside the anger and deal compassionately with the person or situation, without causing more strife.

Oh the peace we could enjoy by letting our anger go, by giving it to God instead of wallowing in it. Toss the acidic, angry grapes. Allow God to transform sour into sweet. Pause and pray.

Prayer: Dear Lord, when I'm angry or irritated, help me to bring my feelings straight to your throne. Guide me in resolving conflicts in a peaceful way. In Jesus' name, Amen.

Grape and Lentil Salad

Ingredients:

1 pound bag of lentils
6 cups water
2 cups seedless grapes, halved
1 medium cucumber, peeled, seeded and diced
2 tablespoons fresh parsley, chopped

Dressing:
1/2 cup olive oil
6 tablespoons lemon juice
2 tablespoons honey
1 teaspoon cumin
1 teaspoon salt

Directions:

Rinse and sort the lentils. Place water and lentils in large pot and bring to a boil. Reduce heat and simmer with pot lid tilted for about 20 minutes. Do not overcook lentils or they will become mushy. Pour lentils into colander, rinse gently with cool water and allow to drain completely. Mix dressing in a glass liquid measuring cup. Microwave dressing for 10 seconds to get honey to dissolve, then stir well. Put lentils, grapes, cucumbers and parsley into a large bowl. Toss with dressing. Keep refrigerated. Makes 8-10 servings.

This recipe tastes even better the next day, so make ahead and refrigerate overnight.

#20
Like an Olive Tree

I am like an olive tree flourishing in the house of God; I trust in God's unfailing love for ever and ever.
Psalm 52:8

Olive trees are incredibly resilient, often living for hundreds of years. They survive tough times like wind and drought by developing deep roots. If the trunk is cut down, a new tree will sprout from the robust, hardy roots.

Throughout history, olive trees have been multi-taskers, supplying necessities of life as well as products that nurture and comfort. In Biblical times, the olive fruit was commonly eaten with meals. Olive oil was used for multiple purposes – to make bread, to flavor other foods, to preserve fish and as fuel for lamps to illuminate the home. It was mixed with spices to make embalming oils and blended with plant components and spices to make perfume.

Olive wood was prized for making furniture because of its strength and beautiful grain. Branches from olive trees were used as symbols of peace and victory. The dove Noah sent from the ark to find land returned carrying an olive branch – symbolic of dry land where the family would begin their new life.

Women are like olive trees. We're strong, resilient and expert multi-taskers. We nurture and comfort others while supplying the essentials of life for our families, friends and coworkers. On a single Saturday we might paint the bathroom, run to the post office, bandage a scraped knee, run one child to piano lessons and another to buy new jeans, then return home to wash laundry and cook dinner. Many days it feels like we're meeting everyone's needs but our own.

I like the thought of being like an olive tree, strong and productive, "flourishing in the house of God." But in order to flourish, I must care for my own needs so that I stay healthy. One way I do that is by utilizing olives and olive oil. It's the only oil I stock in my kitchen for cooking and eating. Did you know that Jesus probably ate olive oil every day?

The health benefits of olives are truly remarkable. They are bursting with disease-fighting compounds like anthocyanins, flavonoids and polyphenols. The polyphenols in olives and olive oil fight inflammation, enhance immune function and help protect DNA from damage. That's quite an impressive resume already, but there's more.

Olives and olive oil contain monounsaturated fats, the good-for-you kind of fats that promote a healthy heart and blood vessels. They also contain vitamin E, beta-carotene and other antioxidants. Whether they're green, black or pressed into oil, those little olives are multi-tasking to keep your body healthy.

I use "extra virgin" olive oil for making marinades, salad dressings and sautéing veggies. Extra virgin olive oil is the highest quality oil from the first pressing of the olives. It isn't heated or refined, which can cause oil to lose some of its health benefits.

Try olive oil for beauty treatment, too. I keep a bottle in the bathroom – it's a soothing alternative to chemical-laden cosmetics and lotions.

Here are a few ways to pamper yourself with olive oil: Give your hair a hot oil treatment. Massage it into your cuticles. Smooth a drop under each eye. Slather generously on your legs after shaving. Apply to lips as moisturizer - if you swallow a little bit, all the better!

Prayer: Dear Lord, thank you for the blessings of the olive tree. Help me to incorporate olives and olive oil into my daily routine to help me flourish as I care for my loved ones. In Jesus' name, Amen.

Zesty Olive Pasta Salad

Ingredients:

1 pound spiral pasta, cooked, drained and cooled
1 large cucumber, peeled and diced
20 large seedless grapes, halved
1 can (6 ounces) black olives, drained and halved
crosswise
1 can (15 ounces) mandarin oranges, drained
2 heaping tablespoons parmesan cheese

Dressing:
1/2 cup extra light tasting olive oil
1/4 cup apple cider vinegar
2 tablespoons water
1 tablespoon orange juice
1 teaspoon fresh orange zest
1 packet Italian salad dressing mix

Directions:

In large bowl, stir together pasta, cucumber, grapes and
olives. Add dressing ingredients to cruet or jar, replace lid and
shake well. Pour half of dressing over pasta mixture and stir
well. Sprinkle parmesan cheese over top and stir again. Gently
fold in mandarin oranges. Bring pasta salad to room
temperature before serving. Makes about 8 servings.

Note: Remainder of dressing can be stored at room
temperature and used on salads.

The blend of sweet oranges and grapes with salty olives and parmesan gives a refreshingly different twist. I use Good Seasons brand salad dressing mix but you could just add garlic and herbs if you prefer.

#21
The Oddball Fruits

Blessed is he who has regard for the weak.
Psalm 41:1a

Most fruits have similar components like fiber, antioxidants and vitamins. They taste juicy and sweet and are essentially fat-free. But there are two oddball fruits - the avocado and the olive. Neither is juicy. Neither tastes sweet. Yet botanically speaking, they are still fruits.

Many people are shocked to learn that avocados and olives are loaded with fat. In fact, the avocado is nicknamed the "butter pear" because of its creamy, butter-like consistency and pear-like shape. Don't let the high-fat content worry you though. Avocados and olives contain monounsaturated fats, the "good-for-you" fats that help lower blood cholesterol.

The oddball fruits are healthful but lack the bright colors and sweet aroma of most fruits. Perhaps that is why you rarely see an avocado in a fruit basket. A can of olives nestled amongst the oranges, apples and pineapple would look especially peculiar, don't you think?

Sometimes people feel like oddballs, too. It's a lonely experience to be in a crowd and yet feel invisible. The Bible tells the story of such a person in John 5. There was a man who had been unable to walk for thirty-eight years. He was lying by a pool that was supposed to cure whichever person stepped into it immediately after the water stirred. But each time the water moved, someone else from the crowd got in first. Why? Because the man had no one to carry him to the pool. No friends, no helpers. He was the odd-man-out, lying there in the crowd, lonely and weak.

One day the man heard a voice speaking to him. He dragged his eyes away from watching the water and looked into the face of Jesus. Can you imagine this poor fellow's joy that someone cared about him? Then Jesus healed him! Because he could walk, the man's days of being an outcast by the pool were over.

Have you ever felt out of place in a crowd? Whether you're eating alone in a restaurant or walking into a meeting where you don't know a soul, it's not a comfortable feeling. It feels good when somebody reaches out to include you.

Jesus made a habit of reaching out to brokenhearted folks and outcasts of society. He hung out with tax collectors and healed blind people and victims of leprosy. He sought out lonely, afflicted souls and tenderly cared for them.

We can be the hands of Jesus in today's world to care for those who feel like oddballs. Everyone has "down" times in life when they feel alone. Loneliness can masquerade as grumpiness. Sometimes a person who complains or makes flippant remarks is simply feeling like the odd-woman-out. She might appreciate being invited out for lunch or shopping.

Sometimes people feel like they no longer fit in as a result of major life changes like divorce or being widowed. Making the transition from a being a couple to a single can be disconcerting. Becoming a single mom can be lonely and overwhelming.

It doesn't matter if fruits are oddballs. But it's a tragedy when people feel excluded and insignificant. Look around at work or in your neighborhood for a person who might feel like an oddball. How could you bless her today?

Prayer: Dear Lord, it hurts my heart to think of people feeling like no one cares. Please lead me to someone who would benefit from a kind word or deed. In Jesus' name, Amen.

Avocado Chow Chow

Ingredients:

1 can (15 ounces) yellow corn, drained
1 can (15 ounces) black beans, rinsed and drained
3 plum tomatoes, finely chopped
1 orange bell pepper, chopped
1 avocado, diced

Dressing:
2 tablespoons balsamic vinegar
2 tablespoons honey
2 teaspoons Dijon mustard
1/4 cup olive oil
1/2 teaspoon salt
1/4 teaspoon pepper

Directions:

Place corn, beans, tomatoes, bell pepper and avocado in a medium bowl. Mix dressing ingredients in a liquid measuring cup and pour over all. Stir well to coat. Serve immediately as a salad or with corn chips as a salsa.

To prepare the day before, mix all ingredients except avocado and refrigerate. Add avocado right before serving and bring salad to room temperature.

#22
Pink Applesauce

*Pleasant words are a honeycomb, sweet to the soul and
healing to the bones.*
Proverbs 16:24

My mom is a wonderful cook, but it's one of the simplest things she makes that my kids like best – pink applesauce. It isn't made from rare, exotic pink apples. It's much easier than that. Mom stirs a handful of red cinnamon heart candies into the warm applesauce until they melt. So simple, yet so special. We enjoy pink applesauce at every holiday dinner.

Why do people like sweet flavors like pink applesauce? Because they're pleasant to the taste buds. Sweetness is comforting and makes us feel good. A love for sweets seems to be innate in humans. Babies are born with a taste for breast milk, which is sweet because it contains a sugar called lactose. Pediatricians recommend introducing baby food vegetables before fruits. The thought is that if fruits are offered first, the baby may prefer their sweetness and refuse the veggies later.

Like the taste buds, our ears prefer sweetness, too, in the form of sweet words. Everyone likes to hear compliments, good wishes, praise and congratulations. We even teach our children to use polite "magic words" like please and thank you.

But what about the words we utter that aren't sweet. What about complaining, arguing, lies and gossip? If they had a flavor, these words would most likely taste sour or bitter. Whether they're sweet or sour, words are the fruit of the tongue. Each of us is responsible for the words we allow past our lips. The problem is, sour and bitter words want to sneak out more frequently than most of us would like.

Proverbs 18:21 says "The tongue has the power of life and death and those who love it will eat its fruit." This verse means that we will reap the consequences of ALL of our spoken words, whether they are sweet or sour. Eating the fruit of sweet words is easy. When we speak pleasant words that build people up, the results are good. But the fallout from bitter words can be unpleasant, even devastating to our relationships. How can we put a muzzle on those pesky unwholesome words?

I learned a lot about the tongue from my friend Mary. When she took her turn leading our mother's group, she taught on the topic of gossip. She passed out a paper listing three questions to ask before speaking: Is what I want to say true? Is it kind? Is it necessary? If the answer to all three questions is yes, then go ahead and say it. If the answer to even one of the questions is "no," then keep quiet.

Sometimes you may have information about someone that is both true and kind, but confidential. For instance, if friends of yours are considering adopting a baby, they should have the privilege of sharing that information with others. So even though it's true and not unkind, it is not necessary for you to tell. Anytime we pass on information that is untrue, unkind or unnecessary, it is gossip.

I want my words to encourage others and build them up, not wound anyone. Like today's verse says, I want my words to be pleasant - sweet to the soul and healing to the bones – like pink applesauce. I must remember to pause and ask: Is it true? Is it kind? Is it necessary?

Prayer: Dear God, may the words of my mouth be acceptable in your sight today. In Jesus' name, Amen.

Pink Applesauce

Ingredients:

1 64-ounce jar applesauce
1/3 cup red cinnamon heart candies
1 teaspoon cinnamon (optional)

Directions:

Pour applesauce into pan and place on medium heat. When applesauce is warm, add candies and stir until they are completely melted. Add cinnamon if desired and mix well.

This makes a pretty side dish for girls' birthday parties. It can be enjoyed warm or cold.

#23
Blossoms, Beauty
and Brain Berries

*Gray hair is a crown of splendor; it is attained by a
righteous life.*
Proverbs 16:31

In the spring, I enjoy looking out my kitchen window at the pretty white blossoms on the apple and pear trees in our backyard. The blossoms are delicate and beautiful, but short-lived. After the blossoms fade and flutter to the ground, tiny outgrowths begin to develop in their places. Over time the tiny fruits take shape up into apples or pears as the sun draws out their rosy and golden hues. Day by day, they gradually ripen into mature fruits filled with good nutrition.

As you and I "ripen" into mature women, we are physically transformed, too. Around forty, give or take a few years, we start to notice little signs of change. Crow's feet. Spots on our hands. Extra pounds that won't budge. A gray hair here and there.

Frankly, it's a little scary. Deep down, many of us feel our worth is tied to our looks. So we wonder, if my outer beauty fades, am I still valuable? Will my coworkers think less of me? Will people whisper at class reunions about how old I look? Will I still be loved? It doesn't seem fair that getting soft and plump is a good thing for fruit but not for us!

Using the word "ripening" instead of aging sounds so much better, doesn't it? When fruit ripens, it improves, getting better with every sun-kissed day. As we ripen, we're getting better, too. With each year we gain more life experience, wisdom and understanding. Our brunette may turn to gray, but our inner beauty flourishes. And as any cancer survivor will tell you, it is a privilege to grow older.

How can we deal with our changing bodies and age gracefully? A good philosophy is "care for the outside but love the inside best." In other words, take whatever steps you can to preserve your outer beauty but realize that inner beauty is the best kind.

"Care for the outside." Instead of expensive plastic surgery or botox treatments, we can choose natural ways to care for our bodies. Antioxidants are a girl's best friend for anti-aging. Keeping a constant supply of antioxidants in your body helps fight inflammation and other damage that leads to disease and signs of aging.

Blueberries are a great place to start - according to current research they possess more antioxidant activity than any other food. Experts coined the nickname "brain berries" because blueberries promote brain health. Eating a cupful daily may slow impairments in motor skills and memory that accompany aging. Plus blueberries contain compounds that fight cancer, reduce inflammation and may even lessen brain damage from strokes.

"Love the inside best." Just as fruit gives its life away to provide sustenance for other creatures, we women give our lives away, too, as we nurture and care for our families. We bear fruit by serving others. We cultivate the godly attributes called fruit of the spirit. These are the quiet sacrifices and prayerful efforts that lead to a deep and lasting inner beauty, whether we're young or well-ripened.

A heart and life that honors God allows our inner beauty to blossom. And these blossoms never fade or fall away. May we come to the place where we see gray hair as God does – as a crown of splendor.

Prayer: Dear Lord, thank you for loving me no matter how I look on the outside. Help me to celebrate the privilege of growing older and cultivate an inner beauty that honors You. In Jesus' name, Amen.

Blueberry Spinach Salad

Ingredients:

5-6 ounce package baby spinach
1 large yellow bell pepper, sliced into thin
1-inch pieces
16 ounces fresh blueberries
1/2 cup dried cranberries
1/2 cup coarsely chopped pecans (optional)

Dressing:
1/3 cup extra virgin olive oil
1/4 cup apple cider vinegar
1 tablespoon prepared yellow mustard
1/3 cup sugar
1 teaspoon celery seed
1/2 teaspoon salt
1/4 teaspoon pepper

Directions:

Toss spinach, pepper, blueberries, cranberries and pecans in large bowl. Mix dressing ingredients in liquid measuring cup and blend well. Drizzle salad with dressing and toss to coat or serve dressing on the side.

The deep colors in this salad make it a beautiful side dish. Add grilled chicken or hard-boiled eggs to serve as an entrée.

#24
Fruity Candy

*All a man's ways seem innocent to him, but motives are
weighed by the Lord.*
Proverbs 16:2

I love gift baskets of candy wrapped in shimmery paper and
tied with a bow. Boxes of colorful, gummy fruit slices are
especially pretty – lemons, oranges and watermelon. They
look too beautiful to unwrap and eat. Each sugary morsel is
filled with...um, well, sugar. And perhaps fat, synthetic dyes
and maybe a few chemical additives and preservatives.

Watermelon-shaped sweets may look like fruit, but they're
just a cheap imitation of the real thing. No vitamins or
antioxidants. No fiber. No real nourishment. The sweet taste of
artificial watermelon flavoring tricks us into thinking it is a
good thing to eat. But as your body digests the sticky glob,
you absorb only empty calories, void of life-sustaining
nutrients.

On the outside, both fruity candy and real fruit are pretty.
But on the inside there's a world of difference. Our reasons for
doing things can be like that, too. Doing things with wrong
motives is like eating fruity candy – it leaves us empty and
unfulfilled. Approaching things with right motives is like
eating real fruit – it nourishes our spirits.

It's easy to think that everything we do is good, especially
if our actions have good results. But that's not how God sees
it. God weighs our motives to determine their value. He sees
deep down into our hearts to the real reasons we do things.

We can fool other people by stating only the selfless

motives we want them to hear. I may tell a friend, "I watched Suzie's kids while she had a root canal. I just wanted to make her unpleasant day a bit brighter." But if the real reason I babysat for Suzie was so she would reciprocate by watching my kids sometime, that's selfish. God knows that and so do I. Claiming the original, sugar-coated reason was counterfeit, just like fruity candy.

In our humanness, it is tough have totally selfless motives. But if we're always thinking of ourselves, we end up using people instead of loving them. That can make us heartsick, just like eating too much candy can make us physically sick. Doing things for the right reasons brings fulfillment and the joy of pleasing God.

How can we have honorable motives? One way is to examine our own hearts and allow God to guide us. Before we say "yes" to any request or opportunity, we need to raise some questions. Do I have time and energy for this or will it overextend me? Would I do it for God's glory or my own? Ask yourself: "Why would I want to do this?" Then make a list of reasons that come to mind.

Pray about the list, asking God to point out any wrong motives. Ask Him to change your heart, creating good motives. Ask for the desire to bless someone or to use your talents for His glory. Or just sit quietly and listen for His direction. Our heavenly Father is thrilled when we yearn for a heart full of pure motives. Don't settle for fruity candy when you can be blessed with real fruit.

Prayer: Dear Lord, I don't want my motives to be fake, like fruity candy. Please change my heart. Give me the desire to do things for the right reasons. In Jesus' name, Amen.

Fruity Oatmeal Cookies

Ingredients:

1 cup butter, softened
1 cup sugar
3/4 cup brown sugar
1-1/2 teaspoons vanilla
2 large eggs
1 cup flour
4 cups old-fashioned oatmeal, divided
1-1/2 teaspoons baking soda
1/2 teaspoon cloves
1 teaspoon cinnamon
1 cup dried cranberries or golden raisins
1 (8-ounce) package chopped dates

Directions:

Place 2 cups oatmeal in food processor and grind to flour-like consistency. Place in large bowl with flour, remaining 2 cups of oatmeal, baking soda, cloves and cinnamon. Mix well and set aside. In a large mixing bowl, cream butter, sugars and vanilla. Add eggs and blend well. Gradually add dry ingredients. Stir in cranberries/raisins and dates. Chill dough for 1 hour.

Drop by spoonfuls onto ungreased cookie sheets. Bake at 350 degrees for about 12 minutes. Cool cookies on wire racks. Makes about 5 dozen (2-1/2 inch) cookies.

The spicy aroma of these cookies baking is heavenly.

#25
A Measure of Faith

...Think of yourself with sober judgment,
in accordance with the measure of faith God has given you.
Romans 12:3b

Life is all about having faith in something. We have faith that the sun will rise each morning. We trust that ocean waves will crash onto the beach and apple trees will produce apples. We have faith the pharmacist will dispense the correct medication and the car will start when we turn the key.

But faith in God is not about rules of nature. It is not about depending on people or machines. Faith is a deep-down confidence that God watches over us. It is knowing He has our best interests in mind and has a plan for our lives.

When you accept Jesus into your heart, God plants a measure of faith within you. That faith gives you strength to trust in God's love and provision, even when you're facing trials or suffering.

Sometimes faith grows quickly when we see God doing marvelous things in our lives. Then there are "slow" times when our faith seems dormant. Those quiet times, when nothing good or bad seems to be happening, are an opportunity to prepare for the next growth spurt.

We can use the quiet times in our faith journey for preparation - like a fruit tree during winter. The tree appears inactive and looks half dead. But deep in the ground, the roots are soaking up nutrients and water, strengthening the tree and preparing it for further growth.

During calm, winter-like times in life, we can allow our roots to go deeper, soaking up knowledge about God and tending to our prayer life. Then when hard times strike, our stronger faith will sustain us and prepare us for further growth.

Remember Joseph and his coat of many colors? His story is an amazing example of strong faith in terrible times. Joseph's jealous brothers threw him in a pit, then sold him to slave traders. He ended up alone, penniless and helpless in a foreign country where he couldn't even speak the language. Can you imagine how horrifying that would be? Joseph had only one thing to hold onto – his faith.

God took care of Joseph. In fact, even the foreigners recognized that he had divine favor. Joseph's boss put him in charge of his whole household. He had a decent life until the boss' wife got him thrown in jail. But even in prison, Joseph was given privileges and responsibilities. After interpreting the Pharaoh's dreams, he ended up second-in-command, saving the nation and his own family from starvation.

In the end, God used Joseph's trials for the benefit of countless people. But think of all the lonely nights, months and years Joseph spent missing his family and wondering what would happen to him. If he had focused on his circumstances, he might have sunk into despair. Instead, he kept his eyes on God and his steadfast faith sustained him.

How is life treating you right now? If things are tranquil, take this opportunity to sink your roots deeper and strengthen your faith. If you're going through a rough patch, take comfort in knowing God is with you. Follow Joseph's example for growing your faith in hard times: Keep your focus on God.

Prayer: Dear Lord, thank you for the gift of faith. Help me to keep my eyes on You when life is more than I can handle. In Jesus' name, Amen.

Double Orange Pork

Ingredients:

4 pork chops, sliced into thin strips
1 cup chopped onion
1 teaspoon fresh ginger, grated
2 tablespoons olive oil
3/4 cup orange juice
1 teaspoon soy sauce
1/2 cup white cooking wine
1 can (15 ounces) mandarin oranges, drained with
juice reserved

Directions:

Stir-fry pork strips in olive oil over medium-low heat until well done. Remove from pan and set aside. In same skillet, increase heat to medium and sauté onion and fresh ginger in olive oil and juices left over from pork. Add orange juice, wine and soy sauce and bring to a boil. Stir cornstarch into 1/4 up of reserved juice from oranges. Slowly add to pan, stirring constantly until sauce thickens. Reduce heat to low. Place pork and oranges into sauce and stir gently until warmed through. Serve over rice or noodles. Serves 4.

A quick and easy way to make pork chops. The sauce is sweet, yet has a nice bite from the ginger. Add more or less ginger to taste.

#26
A Thankfulness Tree

...let us continually offer to God a sacrifice of praise
- the fruit of lips that confess his name.
Hebrews 13:15

As women, we have a bad habit of comparing ourselves to others. There will always be someone who is slimmer or more stylish or a better cook. There will always be things about ourselves and our lives that we would like to change. We can drive ourselves nuts with comparing and nitpicking. Or we can shed the burden of comparison and appreciate the one-of-a-kind masterpieces God designed each of us to be.

Wanting to improve ourselves isn't wrong. Sometimes modifying habits or routines can help us get organized or improve our health. For example, eating more fruit is an easy way to infuse disease-fighting antioxidants into our bodies - a good change. On the other hand, overspending to create "home beautiful" when we need to be saving for a car is probably a bad idea. The trick is figuring out what to change and what to leave alone.

Instead of judging yourself against the proverbial Jones', try comparing your situation to those who are less fortunate. Instead of "I wish my house was bigger," think "Wow, I'm blessed to have two full bathrooms. Many families around the world don't even have indoor plumbing." When you view your home through the lens of the less fortunate, it suddenly seems more than adequate.

Being grateful for our blessings is a powerful antidote to

envious comparisons. When our hearts are thankful, praise naturally flows from our lips. As moms and wives, we can model an attitude of gratitude for our families by voicing our thanks to God. Today's verse says that thankfulness is the fruit of our lips. Living each day in continual praise and thanksgiving chases away feelings of envy and inferiority. Counting blessings can make children feel secure and help them trust in God's provision.

When my kids were little, we used a "Thankfulness tree" to help us tally our blessings. Want to try it? First, shape a trunk and branches from brown construction paper or grocery sacks and mount it on a wall. A roll of brown paper works well, too. Next, trace and cut out lots of leaves from construction paper. We traced a maple leaf and used yellow, orange and red to make an autumn tree. You could use green leaves and cut out apples or pears to make a fruit tree. Each person uses one leaf or fruit per day to write something that they're thankful for. Each day, attach the leaves and fruits to the tree branches with donuts of tape and talk about the blessings. You'll be amazed at how fast your thankfulness tree grows. Doing this with young children is especially fun because they notice miniature blessings we adults might miss such as glittery toothpaste, new crayons and squiggly noodles in their macaroni and cheese.

Concentrating on what we don't have is counterproductive to gratitude. Instead, will you join me in nurturing a habit of thankfulness?

Prayer: Dear Lord, I am so blessed. Keep me focused on the good in myself, my family and our home so that I can model thankfulness to my loved ones. In Jesus' name, Amen.

Strawberry-Banana Salad

Ingredients:

16 ounces of lettuce, torn into bite-sized pieces (5-6 cups)
1 medium cucumber, diced
1/2 pound strawberries, halved or quartered
2 sliced bananas (squirted with lemon juice to prevent browning) and drained

Dressing:
1/4 cup fresh lemon juice
1/4 cup extra light tasting olive oil
1/4 honey
1/2 teaspoon ground ginger
1/4 teaspoon salt
slivered almonds

Directions:

In a liquid measuring cup, mix juice, oil, honey, ginger and salt. Whisk with fork until well-blended. In a large bowl, combine lettuce, cucumbers, strawberries and bananas. Drizzle with dressing and toss to coat. Garnish with slivered almonds and serve immediately. Serves 6-8.

This unique salad makes a tangy accompaniment for chicken and rice.

#27
Raisins of Unforgiveness

If you stand praying, if you hold anything against anyone,
forgive him,
so that your Father in heaven may forgive you your sins.
Mark 11:25

My dog loves bananas. Molly can be sound asleep on the couch and whispering "banana" will bring her awake and alert in a second. The crackle of a banana being opened and peeled brings her running lickety-split from anywhere in the house. Although she eats mostly dry dog food, we make a habit of giving her a tiny bite of banana as a treat.

Fortunately bananas are safe for Molly to eat. But some fruits and vegetables that are perfectly nutritious for humans are deadly for dogs. According to veterinarians, you should never feed your dog grapes or raisins because they can cause kidney failure. Onions and avocadoes are also poisonous to dogs. Giving your dog "just one" grape or raisin occasionally is still unsafe because the toxins can build up and have a cumulative effect over time, leading to illness and even death.

None of us would knowingly give poison to a pet. But sometimes there are things in our own lives that slowly poison us, as if we're a dog eating one raisin at a time. Unforgiveness is one of those things. When we hold grudges and feel offended, resentment becomes a poison that seeps into every area of our lives.

When we don't forgive, it's like having a box of raisins we carry with us. Each time we think about what the other person did to hurt us, it's like eating another raisin. When we mentally replay unpleasant words that were spoken, it's like swallowing another raisin. Over time, the toxins from those "raisins of unforgiveness" build up in our systems, affecting our physical health and leaving our spirits shriveled and bitter.

Why is it so hard to forgive? Sometimes I hold onto unforgiveness because I want the other person to acknowledge the situation and offer an apology. But that's silly - I can't force someone else to apologize. More importantly, in most situations I am partly to blame for whatever conflict occurred, so I need to apologize, too.

Choosing to forgive is always the best option, but it's not always easy. For me, giving up the bitterness is one of those things I have to work at, praying for God's help in releasing the resentment and hurt. It's worth the effort though. Releasing my claim on offenses and giving them to God is a cleansing detox for mind, body and spirit.

Turning an offense over to God unlocks our ability to forgive. We can trust God to handle any situation with our best interests in mind. Being relieved of our burden frees us to forgive the other person.

Forgiving others is not optional. Since God forgives us freely when we do wrong, He expects us to do the same for other people. He doesn't even want us to pray until we've pardoned anyone we "hold anything against." No grudges, no resentment, no ill will of any kind. We are required to let others off the hook first, then God will forgive us.

The act of forgiving has other perks, too. Less mental energy wasted on rehearsing offenses. The ability to love others more fully. More energy to invest in bearing fruit. Plus, ditching toxic emotions feels wonderful and puts a spring in your step.

Is there anyone you need to pardon? Will you dump your "raisins of unforgiveness" and release yourself from their bondage?

Prayer: Dear Lord, bring to mind anyone I need to forgive. Help me to release my hurts and resentments to you so I can receive your blessed forgiveness when I make mistakes. In Jesus' name, Amen.

Note: According to the American Society for the Prevention of Cruelty to Animals, the following "people foods" may be toxic to pets: chocolate, coffee, avocado, grapes, raisins, macadamia nuts, onions, garlic, chives, xylitol, yeast dough.

Golden Fruit Bread

Ingredients:

3 cups bread flour
2 tablespoons wheat gluten
1 package active dry yeast
2 tablespoons brown sugar
2 teaspoons cinnamon
1/4 teaspoon ground ginger
1 cup water
2 tablespoons milk
1 tablespoon olive oil
1/2 cup golden raisins
2 tablespoons candied ginger, minced

The flavor of candied ginger really adds to the uniqueness of this bread but you can substitute 1 teaspoon ground ginger.

Directions:

Grease the pan for your bread machine. Add all ingredients (except raisins and candied ginger) in the order specified by your bread machine directions. If your bread machine has a fruit setting, select that and add the raisins and candied ginger at the signal. If not, use the white bread setting and add raisins and candied ginger partway through the kneading cycle, toward the end.

This sweet bread makes a wonderful peanut butter sandwich. No jelly needed!

#28
Pineapple Pals

*Two are better than one ... if one falls down, his friend can
help him up.*
Ecclesiastes 9a, 10a

While driving the other day, a scene in the front yard of a home caught my eye. Two grown women were sitting side-by-side in the grass, jean-clad legs stretched toward the road, bare feet crossed at the ankles. They had their heads together, talking and laughing while a couple of small children played nearby. The women gave the impression of friends who knew each other well and were totally comfortable in each other's presence. The scene tugged at my heart and made me think of my girlfriends, Paula and Shelley.

The three of us gathered for Bible study for years, starting when our youngest sons were four years old. We took turns meeting at each other's houses each week - studying, chatting and praying while the trio of boys played in another room. The three of us likened ourselves to a three-stranded cord because the time we spent together strengthened us for the week ahead. Like the verse from Ecclesiastes 4:12 says "A cord of three strands is not quickly broken."

In addition to making each other stronger, the three strands of the cord are intertwined, so they know each other intimately. Paula stated this aspect of close friendship one time during our Bible study. She said, "It feels so good to be known!" What Paula meant was that Shelley and I knew her heart. We could listen to a concern she shared and understand it in the context of her life circumstances. The three of us knew nitty-gritty details about each other's fears, dreams, past mistakes and hopes for the future. To know someone that deeply requires spending time together – talking, praying, laughing...even crying.

Our friendships grow when we spend time together. In a similar way, fruits can help each other ripen by hanging out together. If you put a hard avocado in a bag with a ripe apple or banana, the gases given off by the already-ripe fruit will help the avocado to ripen faster. It appears that even fruits need friends!

One fruit is a symbol of friendship. Historically, the pineapple served as a sign of hospitality, friendship and good cheer when used as a centerpiece at colonial dinner parties. Even today, pineapple-shaped brass doorknockers and wall ornaments are popular symbols of hospitality and welcome.

No matter how much we love our friends, sometimes life circumstances change and we can't be together as often. Paula, Shelley and I started out meeting every week for a few years, then switched to every other week for a while. Then Paula started substitute teaching at the local elementary school. I began planning books and writing for magazines and Shelley got busy with various activities and a part-time job. More and more time passed between our get-togethers as our children grew and other responsibilities increased. We still get together, but not nearly as often and I miss our weekly visits.

It's easy to get busy and neglect our friendships. But making time for our girlfriends is essential for us as women. Whether it's face-to-face time or a phone call, keeping connected helps us nurture and fortify each other. Is there a friend you've been missing? Pick up the phone and call her. Or better yet, stop by to surprise your friend with a fresh pineapple and a big hug.

Prayer: Dear Lord, thank you for the blessing of good friends. Help me to take time from my busy schedule to nurture my friendships. In Jesus' name, Amen.

Pineapple Cheese Ball

Ingredients:

2 (8 ounce) packages cream cheese, softened
1 can (8 ounces) crushed pineapple, drained
1/4 cup green pepper, finely chopped
2 tablespoons onion, finely chopped
1/4 teaspoon garlic powder
1 teaspoon seasoning salt
2 cups pecans, finely chopped, divided

Directions:

In large bowl, mix cream cheese, pineapple, green pepper, onion, garlic powder and salt until well-blended. Stir in 1-1/4 cups pecans. Shape into one large ball centered on a decorative plate. Cover with remaining nuts. Chill for 24 hours to allow flavors to blend. Serve with crackers.

A friend of my grandmother's shared this recipe with our family many years ago. Makes a great take-along dish for parties and potlucks.

#29
Fridge Fruit

And we pray this in order that you may live a life worthy of the Lord
and may please him in every way: bearing fruit in every good work...
Colossians 1:10a

Don't you just love a cluttered refrigerator? Everyone loves a nicely stocked fridge on the inside. Especially the fruit drawer! But what's especially lovely is when the outside is overflowing with signs of creativity and love. Crayon drawings, cut-out snowflakes, macaroni mosaics with pieces dropping off each time the door closes – these are the fruit of busy little hands.

Small children love to show their parents what they did at school. Their little faces beam when Mommy or Daddy positions their newest artwork on the refrigerator door and praises them for a job well done. We proudly display their creative gifts, even if falling glitter makes the kitchen floor sparkly for weeks. As the kids grow, pages of fingerpainting are replaced with photos of sports teams and dance recitals.

As parents, we often transform the refrigerator door into an exhibit of good things from our childrens' lives. What if God did the same thing?

Imagine for a moment that there's a huge refrigerator in heaven. As God's children, we are constantly showing our daily work to our heavenly Father. In your mind's eye, visualize God posting pictures of your life's fruit on his fridge.

Each snapshot is a moment from your day capturing the

essence of what you did, whether it was fruitful or not. If you've done a poor job of showing love or mercy to someone, it will show up in your "refrigerator artwork" for the day. When you demonstrate a fruit of the spirit, like patience or kindness, there's the evidence on the fridge. Every action, word and thought captured for God's viewing pleasure.

Perhaps God would write captions under the photos saying things like this:

-Here's a snapshot of my daughter caring for her children when they had the stomach flu. She was so tender and compassionate, even though they threw up all over her new carpet."

-This is when she was irritated and snapped at a coworker. I hope she will do better tomorrow."

-This one shows her taking homemade soup to a neighbor after his surgery, even though he was always unpleasant and even called the police when her dog barked. What a wonderful display of mercy."

-Here is my sweet daughter praying for her own children, day after day after day. I'm so proud of her."

As parents, we treasure the artwork on our refrigerators, even with its imperfections. We don't expect our two-year-old to color in the lines. We don't ask our three-year-old to sketch portraits. We appreciate each child's unique abilities and gifts.

Likewise, God knows we won't always create masterpieces for his fridge. Sometimes our attempts at life's artwork looks more like messy fingerpainting, God still values it. Our job is to do the very best we can to please God.

The neat thing about God's fridge is that he clears off yesterday's work and makes a clean slate each morning. Each day is a new chance for you and me to offer our lives for His approval.

It is truly a privilege to live each day bearing fruit for God. What kind of pictures will you post on His heavenly refrigerator today?

Prayer: Dear Lord, it's my deepest desire to make you proud of my life's artwork. Help me to bear fruit as an offering to you, my heavenly Father. In Jesus' name, Amen.

Creamy Fruit Soup

Ingredients:

4 cups (32 ounces) 100% white grape juice
2 tsp. cornstarch
2 cinnamon sticks
2 whole cloves
1 pound frozen sliced peaches, thawed
1 pound fresh strawberries
1 cup sweetened condensed milk

Directions:

In a large pan, place white grape juice, cornstarch, cinnamon sticks and cloves and bring to a boil. Reduce heat and simmer, uncovered, for 15 minutes. Remove pan from heat and discard cloves. In a food processor, puree one cup of peaches and whisk into hot juice. Allow mixture to cool for 15-20 minutes. Dice strawberries and remaining peaches and add to juice mixture. Whisk in sweetened condensed milk. Cover and chill overnight. Remove cinnamon sticks and stir soup before serving. Serve chilled. Makes 6-8 servings.

Perfect for a ladies' tea. Serve with plain muffins, lady fingers or scones. If you prefer a smooth soup, puree all of the strawberries and peaches.

#30
Fruit for Dessert

*Abigail took two hundred loaves of bread, two skins of wine,
five dressed sheep,
five seahs of roasted grain, a hundred cakes of raisins and
two hundred cakes of pressed figs and loaded them on
donkeys.*
I Samuel 25:18

Do you ever surprise friends or family members with unexpected gifts, for no particular reason? Things like flowers, a card, food – given simply to show your love and appreciation for them. For a whole year, my secret sister at church surprised me periodically with a box of candy, a music CD or other thoughtful gift. Back then I didn't know who the gifts were from, but it was my friend Nelian, who now calls herself my "revealed sister."

There was a woman in the Bible named Abigail who gave a surprise gift that saved the lives of many people. Here's what happened: David and his army were camped out in the desert near the property of Nabal, a rich but foolish man. David sent a few young men to ask Nabal for food, since his men had assisted Nabal by protecting his land and flocks from thieves. But Nabal treated David's men badly and sent them away.

David was furious. He ordered his men to strap on their swords, then took four hundred with him to slaughter Nabal and his household. Fortunately, Nabal's wife, Abigail, heard how poorly her husband had treated David's messengers, so she quickly rode out into the wilderness to meet them with a surprise gift - food. She jumped off her donkey and bowed before David, apologizing for her husband's foolishness. Imagine how shocked David and his hungry men were to see a beautiful woman trekking across the wilderness to bring them a caravan of food-laden donkeys. You can bet their surprise quickly turned to pleasure as they opened sack after sack of provisions.

Abigail knew how to plan a picnic! She packed bread, wine, meat and even dessert. What did she bring for dessert? Raisins and figs. Fruit for dessert. What a wise woman. (You can read the rest of Abigail's story in I Samuel 25.)

I wish I could surprise God with a special gift, like Abigail surprised David. But God is one of those hard-to-buy-for folks. Although it's impossible to surprise God, it IS possible to please Him.

Here are some ways we can please God:

-Hang out with Him. Pray every day, at least for a little while. Go to church for fellowship and to learn more.

-Read His book. The Bible isn't boring. It's full of exciting stories like the one about Abigail and David. Plus it contains lots of practical advice for everyday living.

-Live a fruitful life, doing good things for others. At the same time, keep working on building fruit-of-the-spirit characteristics into your personality. It's a lifelong process, so be patient with yourself along the way.

-Take care of the body He gave you. Eat healthy. Exercise a few times a week. Get enough sleep-

-Take care of your family. Keep the kitchen stocked with healthy options. Encourage them to do all of the above.

Pleasing God is something we can do faithfully, day-in and day-out. Eating fruit each day is a wise habit to cultivate, too. Abigail ended her surprise picnic on a sweet note. Why not follow her example and surprise your family with fruit for dessert tonight?

Prayer: Dear Lord, I want to please you. Help me to live a faithful, fruitful life. In Jesus' name, Amen.

Blackberry Apple Pie

Ingredients:

2 pie crusts
4-5 cups apples, coarsely chopped
2 cups blackberries, fresh or frozen
3/4 cup sugar
3 tablespoons tapioca
1/2 teaspoon cinnamon

Directions:

Core and peel apples, then slice thin. Chop each slice into
4-5 pieces. Place apples and blackberries in a large bowl. Mix
sugar, tapioca and cinnamon together and stir into fruit until
coated. Allow to sit for 15 minutes. Spoon fruit into pastry-
lined pie dish. Top with second crust and crimp edge. Cut slits
in top and cover crust edges with pie crust shield or strips of
aluminum foil. Bake at 400 degrees for 40 minutes. Remove
shield/foil and bake for 20 minutes more or until crust is
golden brown. Makes 8 servings.

*A nice twist on plain apple pie. I prefer using frozen berries
because they don't break apart when stirring with the sugar
mixture.*

Fruit Lovers' Devotions to Go